THE BASIC
ENGLISH
HANDBOOK

THE BASIC ENGLISH HANDBOOK

Gilbert H. Muller

Fiorello H. LaGuardia Community College
of the City University of New York

HARPER'S COLLEGE PRESS

A Department of Harper & Row, Publishers

New York   Hagerstown   San Francisco   London

Sponsoring Editor: *Paula White*
Project Editor: *Richard T. Viggiano*
Designer: *Frances Torbert Tilley*
Production Supervisor: *Kewal K. Sharma*
Compositor: *Bi-Comp, Incorporated*
Printer and Binder: *The Murray Printing Company*
Art Studio: *Vantage Art Inc.*
Cover painting: *Frances Torbert Tilley*

THE BASIC ENGLISH HANDBOOK
Copyright © 1978 by Gilbert H. Muller

Library of Congress Cataloging in Publication Data

Muller, Gilbert H   Date-
  The basic English handbook.

  Includes index.
  1. English language—Grammar—1950-   2. English
language—Rhetoric.   I. Title.
PE1112.M8   808'.042   77-14267
ISBN 0-06-160424-0

ACKNOWLEDGMENTS

I am grateful to Alan Berman and Irwin Feder of LaGuardia Community College for their advice and assistance in preparing the business writing section of this book. I also wish to thank LaGuardia Professors Mary Lee Abkemeier and John Hyland for their helpful comments on the science and social science chapters.

Grateful acknowledgment is also made for the use of the following material. Page 20: the cartoon "Hereafter," copyright by Clarence Brown; page 38: the "Peanuts" cartoon, © 1975 United Feature Syndicate, Inc.; page 155: from "The Changing Place of Women in America," by Carl N. Degler, reprinted by permission of the publisher, *Daedalus;* page 170: the diagram "Original Graphic Arts Process" © American Home Publishing Company, Inc.; p. 177: from *Understanding English* by Paul Roberts, copyright © 1958 by Paul Roberts, by permission of Harper & Row, Publishers; page 202: reprint of page from *Reader's Guide to Periodical Literature,* Copyright © 1971, 1972. Material reproduced by permission of The H. W. Wilson Company; p. 214: from *In Our Time* by Ernest Hemingway, reprinted by permission of the publisher, Charles Scribner's Sons; page 218: "Proletarian Portrait," by William Carlos Williams, from *Collected Earlier Poems,* copyright 1938 by New Directions Publishing Corporation. Reprinted by permission of New Directions Publishing Corporation.

CONTENTS

PART 2 The Sentence: Putting Words Together 43

PREFACE

The Basic English Handbook is a complete text for entry level writing courses. Designed as a practical guide to composition, it seeks to help people write effectively in a variety of college and job situations.

This text has been designed to stress the key skills required in sound writing. Part 1 concentrates on vocabulary development, and on the accurate selection of words. Part 2 assists students in the mastery of grammar, mechanics, and sentence structure. It offers practical advice on solving the major grammatical problems evident in much college writing today. Part 3 deals with the process of organizing and developing paragraphs and essays; students will be able to move systematically from the point where thinking about the topic actually begins to the presentation of the final written product. Part 4 is a unique section on applied writing for courses and jobs, including information on the short research paper, technical writing, writing for literature, science, and social science courses, preparing for examinations, proofreading and revision, and submitting papers in proper manuscript form. Thus *The Basic English Handbook* guides students gradually from the simplest elements of writing to applications for everyday life.

Throughout, prescriptive material is kept to a minimum and inductive mastery of skills is stressed. Teachers will find a blend of traditional and contemporary examples selected to appeal to a broad student audience. Exercises that reinforce writing skills appear at the end of each chapter, and there is ample space for answering questions in the text itself.

The Basic English Handbook permits flexible use by teachers and students alike. Teachers of remedial writing will want to concentrate heavily on the first two parts of the text, while teachers of basic composition might prescribe individual chapters from these sections as the need arises while focusing on paragraph and essay development in Part 3. Instructors can create workshop situations or encourage individualized learning by permitting students to move through the text at their own pace, checking with the teacher once a specific chapter has been completed. Finally, where there is a strong business or technical thrust to the college curriculum, teachers will want to discuss relevant chapters in Part 4.

Because it is a student-centered text that offers practical advice in an easy-to-follow manner, *The Basic English Handbook* can be used by students on their own without difficulty. Students can locate information readily by consulting both the table of contents and the index, by following the page tabs, by relying on numerous cross-references and handy boxed "hints," and by consulting the charts and correction symbols on the inside covers. Once they have located relevant information, they will be pleased to discover that it can be understood. The aim has been to keep the style relaxed and lively, the language simple without being condescending, the type readable, and the page layouts clear and uncluttered.

As college teachers today, we are faced with dramatic weaknesses in student writing. Many major handbooks that have been on the market for a number of years fail to address the rudimentary nature of these problems in a manner that is comprehensible to students with persistent writing difficulties. *The Basic English Handbook* aims to meet the needs and expectations of such students and seeks to make the craft of writing manageable for all people who must learn to write for achievement in academic and vocational contexts.

G.H.M.

CORRECTION SYMBOLS

SYMBOL	MEANING	REFER TO CHAPTER
Abr	Unnecessary or incorrect abbreviation	25
Abst	Too abstract; use concrete words	3
Adj	Wrong form of adjective	13, 22
Adv	Wrong form of adverb	13, 22
Agr	Error in noun or pronoun agreement	16, 21
Apos	Misused apostrophe; apostrophe needed	25
Awk; K	Awkward phrasing or sentence structure	13, 14
Cap	Capital letter needed	25
No cap	No capital letter required	25
Cl?	Unclear; explain	
Cliché	Overused expression	7
Coh	Coherence lacking	28
Colloq	Too colloquial; use written English	5
Conc	Weak conclusion	29, 35
Coord	Faulty coordination	19
CS	Comma splice	18
D	Mistake in diction	6
Dev	Ideas must be further developed	28
Dg	Misplaced or dangling modifier	19
Dict	Consult a dictionary	1
Div	Improper division of word at end of sentence	25
Euph	Do not use euphemistic language	10
Frag	Sentence fragment	17
Gen	Word selection is too general; use more specific vocabulary	4
Gr	Error in grammar	13
H	Misused homonym	11
Intro	Weak introduction	27, 33

∧	Add the following
ℓ	Delete (eliminate)
∿	Transpose (reverse the order)
◡	Close up space

TO THE WRITER

Good writing—like effective speaking—is a basic source of communication for all of us. It permits us to share experiences, emotions, information, and ideas. Yet you might ask, "Why write? I can get through life without it." Perhaps you can avoid the need to write, to a large extent. But this is somewhat like saying that you can get through life without ever taking a bath; without ever loving someone; without ever accepting a challenging task. What is the value of such an attitude, and what do you become?

There will be many times when you simply have to write well. For one thing, you have to write properly in order to pass many courses. This is true even for subjects other than English; more and more teachers are refusing to grade for "content" alone and are now demanding sound writing from students. Competent writing ability also contributes to your success in the business world. Frequently you have to write autobiographical essays on job applications. Moreover, once you have a job, you will have to apply effective writing skills in a variety of work situations. And if you expect to advance in your job, you should remember that many promotion tests, including those administered by the Civil Service, require the writing of paragraphs and essays. Clearly then, there are payoffs in college and in work for people who can write well. Effective writing is something that you can take pride in, but it is also a decidedly practical skill.

The Basic English Handbook is a reference guide—a map of sorts—to those basic skills that are needed for sound college writing and in writing beyond college. Unlike many other English handbooks on the market, it is not complicated. The organization of the *Handbook* is clear and simple, moving from vocabu-

1

lary, to sentences, to paragraphs and essays, and finally to forms of writing for courses and jobs. The writing is direct and is designed to provide you with information that can be readily understood. You should be able to use this *Handbook* with ease.

Many English teachers will ask you to move through the *Handbook* chapter by chapter, thereby using it as the foundation of a complete course in writing. Other teachers will assign sections which they feel will aid you in strengthening specific writing skills. You can also use the *Handbook* on your own because it has not been designed exclusively for English courses, but for a variety of writing assignments that you might have to undertake.

Regardless of the manner in which you utilize *The Basic English Handbook,* you will want to address yourself to the exercises in each section. These exercises have been planned not only to provide practice in order to improve writing performance, but also to allow you to discover something about yourself and your language. Space has been provided so that you can write answers to these exercises in the text. Thus you can create a single source for all your writing activities, rather than use random sheets that are often unsightly and easily lost.

Many experts have pointed to the recent decline in writing abilities among Americans of all ages, but especially among college students. This text will not reverse the trend in declining English standards. However, it can prevent *you* from serving as a statistic within this gloomy picture of writing quality in the United States. *The Basic English Handbook* has been designed to meet your fundamental writing needs and expectations.

PART 1

VOCABULARY:
Working with Words

There is an argument in *Alice in Wonderland* that focuses, as does much of this famous book, on the nature of words:

"But 'glory' doesn't mean a 'nice knock-down argument,' " Alice objected.

"When I use a word," Humpty Dumpty said in a rather scornful tone, "it means just what I choose it to mean—neither more nor less."

"The question is," said Alice, "whether you can make words mean so many different things."

"The question is," said Humpty Dumpty, "which is to be master—that's all."

Perhaps we envy Humpty Dumpty, who uses words any way he wants. However, there are limits to the meaning of any given word. Sometimes we can be totally wrong in the way we use a word. At other times, we can be just slightly off the mark. Humpty Dumpty attempts to be the ruler of words by inventing his own definitions for them. We can be masters of words only in the sense that we can learn their existing meanings. A word cannot mean too many things, although it can certainly possess shades of meaning. The starting point in effective writing is to know, as does Alice, that "glory" does *not* mean "a nice knock-down argument." How to use words properly and successfully is the subject of Part One.

CHAPTER 1

The Dictionary

The dictionary is a valuable resource in working with words, and the one text that should serve as a companion for this *Handbook*. It might surprise you to learn that you are probably familiar with anywhere from 20,000 to 100,000 words. These words are termed your *recognition vocabulary*—words that you can recognize when reading. However, your *active vocabulary*—the words that you actually use in conversation and writing—is considerably smaller, one-third or less of your recognition vocabulary. One of your major goals in composition should be to expand the range of active words available to you. A dictionary will help you in this task.

Dictionaries explain the way in which words are used at a given time. To an extent, they provide "rules" for the proper use of words, but dictionaries also reveal that words change in meaning and also in the contexts, or situations, in which they can be employed. Moreover, although most dictionaries make changes and additions on a yearly basis, they rarely account for the most current words we use—words like *Afro, mammography, headshop, water bed,* and *paraprofessional.* (Check an available dictionary to see if any of these words appear in it.) What a good dictionary will do is provide a ready guide to the correct application of a word that has been around for awhile.

1.1. Choosing a Dictionary

There are two main types of dictionaries: *unabridged* works that contain a majority of the approximately 500,000 words in the English language; and *abridged* works that contain only the most commonly used words. Because they are expensive and bulky, unabridged (or un-shortened) dictionaries are more likely to be found in libraries. Abridged dictionaries are easier to carry and more moderately priced; they are the sort that we would keep on the desk, bring to class, or use at work.

The best unabridged dictionaries are

New Century Dictionary of the English Language
New Standard Dictionary of the English Language
The Oxford English Dictionary
The Random House Dictionary of the English Language
The Shorter Oxford English Dictionary
Webster's Third New International Dictionary
World Book Dictionary

Libraries should have these dictionaries in their reference rooms. *Webster's New International* is probably best for the general reader.

As for abridged dictionaries, many are available. Here are the best:

American Heritage Dictionary
Random House Dictionary
Standard College Dictionary
Thorndike-Barnhart Comprehensive Desk Dictionary
Webster's New World Dictionary of the American Language
Webster's New Collegiate Dictionary

In addition to these abridged dictionaries, there are even shorter paperback dictionaries that are especially valuable for classroom use. These paperback dictionaries do not give a complete range of meanings for words, but even in their simplified form they permit you to check basic meanings and the spelling of a word. The most frequently used paperback dictionary is the *New Merriam Webster Pocket Dictionary*. If you purchase this dictionary, you can be certain that it is up to date.

1.2. Using the Dictionary.

Once you have selected a dictionary, you should familiarize yourself with the "front matter" and with any supplementary material that comes after the entries. The front matter is a guide to the correct use of the dictionary and will enable you to better handle the information given you in an entry. The supplementary material provides valuable lists on opposite page and tables of practical information. The Table of Contents from *Webster's New World Dictionary*[1] suggests the range of information that a good dictionary will make available to you.

---

[1] Reprinted with permission. From *Webster's New World Dictionary of the American Language,* College Edition. Copyright © 1962 by The World Publishing Company.

CONTENTS

The bulk of the dictionary consists of entries, or words listed in the text. Here is a sample entry:[2]

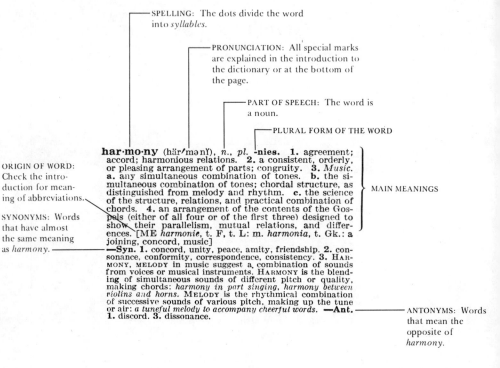

SPELLING: The dots divide the word into *syllables*.

PRONUNCIATION: All special marks are explained in the introduction to the dictionary or at the bottom of the page.

PART OF SPEECH: The word is a noun.

PLURAL FORM OF THE WORD

ORIGIN OF WORD: Check the introduction for meaning of abbreviations.

SYNONYMS: Words that have almost the same meaning as *harmony*.

har·mo·ny (här′mə nY), *n., pl.* **-nies. 1.** agreement; accord; harmonious relations. **2.** a consistent, orderly, or pleasing arrangement of parts; congruity. **3.** *Music.* **a.** any simultaneous combination of tones. **b.** the simultaneous combination of tones; chordal structure, as distinguished from melody and rhythm. **c.** the science of the structure, relations, and practical combination of chords. **4.** an arrangement of the contents of the Gospels (either of all four or of the first three) designed to show their parallelism, mutual relations, and differences. [ME *harmonie*, t. F, t. L: m. *harmonia*, t. Gk.: a joining, concord, music] **—Syn. 1.** concord, unity, peace, amity, friendship. **2.** consonance, conformity, correspondence, consistency. **3.** HARMONY, MELODY in music suggest a combination of sounds from voices or musical instruments. HARMONY is the blending of simultaneous sounds of different pitch or quality, making chords: *harmony in part singing, harmony between violins and horns.* MELODY is the rhythmical combination of successive sounds of various pitch, making up the tune or air: *a tuneful melody to accompany cheerful words.* **—Ant. 1.** discord. **3.** dissonance.

MAIN MEANINGS

ANTONYMS: Words that mean the opposite of *harmony*.

As you see, this typical dictionary entry gives you the following information:

1. The *spelling* of a word
2. The *pronunciation* of a word
3. The *meaning* of a word
4. The *part of speech* (noun, verb, adjective) of a word, including related information on such inflected forms as the principal parts of verbs
5. The *origin* of a word—that is, where the word comes from
6. *Synonyms* (words of similar meaning) and *antonyms* (words of opposite meaning) for a word

These are the major functions of an entry, but an entry can also inform you about words typically used in speech, "old-fashioned" or archaic words, variant spellings, and abbreviations—in short, give you a full range of information about any vocabulary item.

[2] From *The American College Dictionary* (New York: Random House, 1962), p. 552.

1.3. The Thesaurus: A Special Dictionary

The *thesaurus* is a special type of dictionary that lists synonyms and antonyms. A good dictionary will provide the same function, but not as extensively as a thesaurus. A typical entry in a thesaurus looks like this:[3]

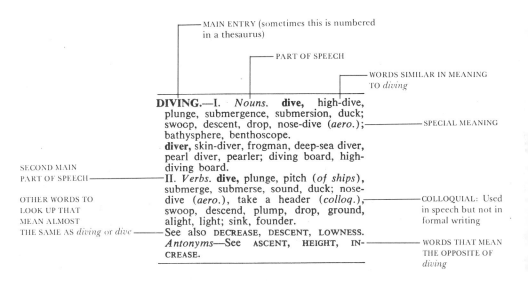

This entry is from *The New Roget's Thesaurus in Dictionary Form*—the most commonly used thesaurus. (The organization of a thesaurus will vary considerably from compiler to compiler.) Although a thesaurus will provide you with a rich assortment of words that are alike or different in meaning, you should be aware that its primary function is to remind you of words that you already know. It does not perform all the work in word selection for you, and you are likely to misuse a word if you encounter it for the first time in a list of synonyms. Make certain that you understand the connotations of any word that you select from a thesaurus (see Section 2).

Application 1   Review the dictionary you have chosen to use and answer the following questions about it.

a. What is its exact title? Does it tell you anything about its nature and scope? _____

_____

---

[3] From *The New Roget's Thesaurus in Dictionary Form* (New York: G. P. Putnam's Sons, 1964), p. 156.

b. What is the most recent copyright date (which can be found on the back of the title page)? _____

c. What special sections appear in the introduction to the dictionary? What information do these sections contain? _____

_____

d. What supplements, if any, appear at the end of the dictionary?

_____

Application 2   Select a word from your dictionary and answer the following questions about it.

a. What language(s) does the word come from? _____

b. How many syllables (single units of sound, which help to determine pronunciation and when to hyphenate) are in the word? _____

c. What part(s) of speech is the word? _____

d. If the word has more than one syllable, which part receives the greatest emphasis in pronunciation? _____

e. How many definitions are there for the word? _____

Application 3   The following synonyms are taken from one entry in *Roget's Thesaurus*. Discuss the meaning of each word and say what part of speech it is. Consult your dictionary if necessary.

a. convolution _____

b. scalloped _____

c. meander _____

d. labyrinth _____

e. undulation _____

f. buckle _____

g. serpentine _____

CHAPTER 2

Total Meaning: Denotation and Connotation

All words have precise, agreed-upon definitions. This is called *denotation*. At the same time, words have "shades of meaning" that dictionaries rarely treat. We bring emotions, associations, and impressions to words, and this is what we mean by *connotation*. For instance, what colorful and vivid feelings do you associate with the following words:

rose
garbage

As you see, some words are rich in their suggestiveness. How, then, do you select a word which communicates precisely what you mean?

Hint: In choosing a word, you have to be aware of the combined denotative and connotative effect it might have on the reader or listener.

Suppose you, in a paper on Kareem Abdul Jabbar (the star center of the Los Angeles Lakers), want to explain his frequent criticism of basketball officiating. You might term his attitude "critical," "sarcastic," "disparaging," "contemptuous," "abusive," or "condemnatory." Denotatively, all these words define Jabbar's negative attitude toward some basketball referees. Yet the words differ connotatively, and consequently alter your total meaning, as well as your own opinion of Jabbar. Select a word that *you* would employ to express both Jabbar's attitude and the fact that you agree with him.

From a slightly different perspective, let's assume that you want to capture Jabbar's height by using a colorful comparison (sometimes termed a "figurative" comparison). You could compare him to a "giant," a "giraffe," a "skyscraper," a "minaret." Each word conveys the idea of extreme tallness, but again its connotation changes the effect it can have on us. Why, for instance, might it be appropriate to equate Jabbar with a "minaret"? What emotional and mental associations do you connect with this word? Of course, if the reader is uncertain about the meaning of *minaret,* all of the connotation will be lost. If he or she connects it only with a lofty tower in a mosque, there will be some connotative effect, but still not all that might have been intended. You always have to consider how much your audience knows, and what its attitudes are, before choosing a word.

Sometimes, there is so much emotional connotation in a word that we tend to lose sight of its denotation, or exact meaning. In "All in the Family," Archie Bunker is so uncomfortable with the word *sex* that he either spells it or refuses to use it at all. On another level, advertisers and politicians have long been aware of the extreme connotative value of certain words and have used them to evoke feelings of approval or dislike. Such words as *bad breath, motherhood, patriotism,* and *communism* are in this category. We should not imitate those who exploit such words. When we use a word like *patriotism,* we should not let excessive emotion obscure its precise meaning.

Application 1 Provide a dictionary definition (denotation) for the following words, and then connotations for each one.

a. rainbow *Definition:* _____

                Connotations: _____

b. pig *Definition:* _____

            Connotations: _____

c. colored *Definition:* _____

                Connotations: _____

d. hippie *Definition:* _____

               Connotations: _____

e. dictator *Definition:* _____

                Connotations: _____

Application 2 List five words that you think evoke very strong feelings of approval or dislike. Be prepared to analyze the denotative and connotative aspects of these words.

a. _____

b. _____

c. _____

d. _____

e. _____

Application 3   Explain why the italicized words in the sentences below, while denotatively correct, could create inappropriate connotations for a reader. Check your dictionary if necessary.

a. I am pleased by your *radical* improvement in the course. _____

_____

b. The priest *rambled* down the aisle. _____

_____

c. I wanted to go to the movies, but my friend *abhorred* the idea. ____

_____

d. The cruel tyrant *chastised* the prisoner. _____

_____

e. She decided to *spurn* the very attractive offer and seek another job.

_____

_____

Application 4   Bring to class examples of connotative language found in advertisements. (Example: "You've come a long way, Baby.") Explain the emotional impressions created by the connotative words and expressions that you have located.

CHAPTER 3

Concrete and Abstract Words

There are words (like *boat, Chicago, magazine,* and *Martin Luther King*) that we call "concrete" because they refer to objects, people, and places. They are concrete in the sense that they can be seen and touched. Concrete words tend to be sensory, reflecting a familiar world that does not confuse the reader when we use such vocabulary. On the other hand, there are words that have "abstract" denotations. Words like *love, wisdom, patriotism, justice,* and *sin* are in this category. Abstract words deal with concepts and ideas; their denotation cannot be grasped or measured easily.

Concrete words tend to take care of themselves, but we have to be careful when we use abstract words. For instance, we all have a general notion of what "love" is, but as an abstract idea it needs clarification. We cannot avoid abstract words, nor should we, because ideas are essential to the craft of writing. Still, we should not heap abstraction upon abstraction, because this makes for dull and frequently fuzzy writing.

> **Hint:** Bring abstract language down to earth by providing concrete illustrations of the concept or idea.

George Orwell, in a famous essay "Politics and the English Language," says that modern language actually is moving away from the concrete toward the abstract and that this should be a subject of concern to everyone who values clear meanings in a complicated world. One example that Orwell gives of abstract language comes from an essay on psychology:

> On the one side we have the free personality: by definition it is not neurotic, for it has neither conflict nor dream. Its desires, such as they are, are transparent, for they are just what institutional approval keeps in the forefront of consciousness; another institutional pattern would alter their number and intensity; there is little in them that is natural, irreducible, or culturally dangerous.

We should not be embarrassed by an inability to understand this passage. The language is so abstract that it actually *hinders* understanding. This is abstract vocabulary on the verge of collapse. Because there is nothing concrete in this passage, we learn little about the main subject, which is the "free personality."

Compare the writing in the Orwell passage with this paragraph by Edith Hamilton, taken from "The Lessons of the Past":

Basic to all the Greek achievement was freedom. The Athenians were the only free people in the world. In the great empires of antiquity—Egypt, Babylon, Assyria, Persia—splendid though they were, with riches beyond reckoning and immense power, freedom was unknown. The idea of it never dawned in any of them. It was born in Greece, a poor little country, but with it able to remain unconquered no matter what manpower and what wealth were arrayed against her. At Marathon and at Salamis overwhelming numbers of Persians had been defeated by small Greek forces. It had been proved that one free man was superior to many submissively obedient subjects of a tyrant.

Notice that the subject—freedom—is the same in both passages. However, Hamilton makes it concrete by relating it to people, nations, and places. Even if we do not know a great deal about countries like Assyria or about famous battles, we do develop an idea about freedom from the concrete manner in which Hamilton connects it with a particular example of the Greek people. If we want to know something about the "free personality," we could find it in Hamilton's statement, but certainly not in the first passage, which has numerous problems in its abstract design.

Hamilton's passage should serve as a model for dealing with abstractions. Do not deliberately confuse a reader by writing on a purely abstract level. Try to isolate just one abstraction, and then root it to people, places, and things.

Application 1 Take one abstraction (like "freedom," "love," "justice," "oppression") and explain it as concretely as possible in a short paragraph of four or five sentences.

_____

_____

_____

Application 2   Locate examples of abstract writing that are troublesome because they lack any concrete base in people, objects, or places. Take one such passage that is relatively short and rewrite it in more concrete language.

_____

_____

_____

_____

_____

_____

_____

_____

CHAPTER 4

General and Specific Words

Just as you should use concrete vocabulary as much as possible, you should also attempt to be specific in your selection of words. A *specific word* is one that is limited in the objects, actions, or qualities it applies to. It is precise, accurate, and definite in its meaning. On the other hand, a *general word* is broad, uncertain, and not clearly focused in meaning. General words take in too much meaning and should be used sparingly in writing.

The nature of specific and general language can be considered in terms of a "generality triangle," turned upside down and showing the way that meanings become more specific as we limit the territory that they cover.

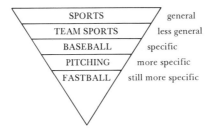

We can see the value of being specific by looking at the following sentences:

General Nolan Ryan is a good ballplayer.

Specific Nolan Ryan's fastball, clocked at over 100 miles per hour, makes him the fastest pitcher in baseball history.

The first example is dull, imprecise, and lifeless in its generality. With the second example, there is a specific meaning and a far more vivid effect.

Hint: Breathe life and meaning into your writing by using specific words.

In conversation, however, we do not always have time to find the most specific word. For instance, if we are asked about a dance that we attended, we might reply, "It was enjoyable." We tend to use the first word that develops in our mind, and often this word is a generality. One major difference between speaking and writing is that with writing we do have the time to be more specific. We can think about the precise word that we want to use, and we can consult a dictionary or thesaurus for help. Consequently, there is no excuse for excessively general word selection in writing.

Application 1 Create a "generality triangle" for one of the following words: *animal, building, automobile, dance, crime.* Try to locate as many stages of specificity in your triangle as possible.

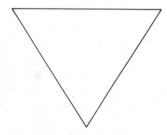

Application 2 Revise the following sentences so that the words are more specific.

a. Most movie actors are good-looking. _____

_____

b. The college could improve its course offerings. _____

_____

c. Vacations are a good thing. _____

_____

d. There are problems in using some types of contraceptives. _____

_____

e. Numerous aspects of the film were criticized by the reviewer. ____

_____

CHAPTER 5

The Vocabulary of Speech: Colloquialisms, Slang, and Dialect

There are many words and expressions that are more appropriate to spoken than written English. These spoken words fall into such categories as *colloquialisms* (words used by a general audience in conversation but not in writing), *slang* (conversational words used by subgroups of people but not by a general audience), and *dialect* (spoken language peculiar to a region, social group, community, or occupational group). Spoken language is in the mainstream of American life, probably moreso today than written English. Moreover, it is increasingly difficult to distinguish between words that are colloquial, slang, and dialect; for instance, words like *jive* and *jazz* have belonged to all three categories, with *jazz* also becoming an accepted word in written English.

What we mean by "written English" is simply that variety of English which is found in newspapers, books, magazines, and other forms of print. (Television has its own form of English, blending spoken and written forms, which some experts term "network standard.") It is removed from the everyday English that we speak and hear because it does not readily admit slang, dialect, and colloquialisms. In certain ways, written English does not reveal as much about ourselves, our origins, and our customs as does spoken English. Nevertheless, written English is the most commonly understood variety throughout the world. It is international English, and what the reading audience expects to see.

> *Hint:* Use colloquialisms, dialect, and slang sparingly in writing in order to add color or emphasize a point.

Words like *plain talk, stinking, gearing up, cracking down,* and *in a bind* are typical of the colloquialisms that most of us are familiar with in conversation. As a more specialized colloquial form, slang would include such words as *bones* (from the world of gambling), *legal beagle* (from the law profession), and *eighty-six* (from construction). The average person may not be familiar with the many varieties of slang in this country, a fact borne out by the difficulty which visitors from abroad have in understanding Americans who use a lot of slang. Many groups have unique slang vocabularies, as is shown in the following diagram:

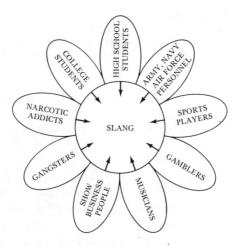

Just as yesterday's slang word becomes today's colloquialism (for instance, *jerkwater town* was once a term that only railroad men and women would have understood), the dividing line between slang and dialect is also somewhat uncertain. *Klootchman* (meaning "a woman," a Chinook Indian term) is clearly dialect, but what are we to make of *reckon, you all, loco, pardner, bamboozle, look-see,* and *what-not,* which are dialect words that have worked their way into the vocabulary of many Americans. The one thing that we can say about dialect in attempting to distinguish it from other spoken forms of English is that it operates through special princi-

ples of grammar and sentence structure, a point discussed in Part 2 of this *Handbook*.

Good writers know how to use spoken English effectively in writing, and articles in magazines like *Rolling Stone* and *The Harvard Lampoon* reflect the vitality and usefulness of spoken varieties of English. In your own writing, use spoken English cautiously. Don't overuse words like *main man* and put quotation marks around colloquialisms to show that you are using them for special effect. (For instance, "The Watergate defendants have been quite successful in 'beating the rap.'") Your audience and the effect which you are seeking should determine your application of spoken English in any given composition.

Application 1   Look again at the diagram on American slang (p. 20). Select one category and then list as many slang words as you can for it. How many of these slang words have developed into colloquialisms understood by most Americans?

_____

_____

_____

Application 2   Rewrite the following paragraph so that all "spoken" language is replaced by commonly accepted written English.

There are pros and cons to abortion, but we should stay cool when rapping about it. What's O.K. for one chick might not go down very well with another. The "right to life" bunch sort of use scare tactics on you, with batches of blown-up pics showing gross fetuses. On the other hand, the pro-abortion crowd makes it sound like it's no big deal. Whatever: in the final analysis, women are in less of a fix today than they were ten years back.

_____

_____

_____

_____

_____

Application 3   Try to establish the origins and meanings of the words listed below. Consult unabridged works like *The Oxford English Dictionary* and specialized sources like *The Dictionary of Americanisms*.

a. *Mafia* _____

_____

b. *vamoose* _____

_____

c. *schlemiel* _____

_____

d. *squaw* _____

_____

e. *pone* _____

_____

CHAPTER 6

Fancy Words: Overblown Diction

In a way, fancy words are the reverse of colloquial words. They are words that are overblown, that are excessively formal, that seemingly are used for their own sake rather than for exact meaning. Ernest Hemingway called such words "twenty-dollar words" and refused to use them in his own writing.

Fancy Words   The execrable nature of the provender, replete with dubious ingredients, caused extreme consternation among the patrons.

Simple Words   The guests were concerned about the poor quality of the food.

Which of the above sentences is clearer to you? Which is shorter? What does this tell you about the dangers involved in using too much fancy language?

> *Hint:* Overuse of big or fancy words leads to overwriting, misuse, and mixed levels of style.

Although it is important to expand your vocabulary, don't use fancy words to excess. A plain, simple style in many instances is far more effective than a style that relies on twenty-dollar words.

Application   Tone down the fancy vocabulary (some of which is misused) in the following sentences. Consult a dictionary for the precise meaning of any word that is unfamiliar to you.

a. In the halcyon epoch of the Civil Rights crusade, Black Studies sequences proliferated in academe. _____

_____

b. Lofty and imperious in demeanor, Daniel Patrick Moynihan is the prototype of the politician as mandarin. _____

_____

c. The architectonic of drag racing mandates a persona that dissociates devotees of the sport from more plebian strains of humanity.

_____

_____

d. Canines leave offal and detritus on a municipality's thoroughfares.

_____

_____

e. Agrarian endeavors inculcate a reverence for pastoral modes of existence. _____

_____

CHAPTER 7

Dead Words: Clichés

Words that are "dead" are called clichés. They are words that were once fresh and lively, but which have literally been worn out or killed off because of overuse. Such words and expressions are also termed "trite." We tend to rely on clichés in conversation, although they certainly are not impressive to careful listeners. We are so familiar with dead vocabulary that we can complete these expressions easily:

far and few _____

too funny for _____

busy as a _____

last but not _____

give me liberty or give me _____

Notice how mechanical our response to dead language is. Yet try to imagine the first time that a person used the expression "too funny for words." That remark must have been considered impressive and original. However, through overuse it has turned into a stock expression. We do not think about it, and we are not impressed by it any more than a reader will be.

> **Hint:** Good writing avoids overworn words, phrases, and popular expressions.

Many words, comparisons, slogans, famous quotations, expressions, and even ideas ("Women are the weaker sex") have lost their vitality in writing. Admittedly, it is difficult for those just starting to perfect their style to avoid clichés entirely. Certain words and phrases are so rooted in our daily vocabulary that it would be awkward to eliminate them. Tech-

Cliché

nically, we would have to characterize the following written expressions as clichés:

the threat of nuclear destruction
fatherly type
Education is a key to success.
worthy opponent
time and time again

Although there might be a shred of life left in some of these phrases, clearly too much writing of this sort creates a problem because it lacks freshness.

Develop an eye for clichés—an ability to recognize stale language in conversations, television programs, and public speeches. Also learn to recognize clichés in your own speech and writing. Don't treat clichés as if they were the "staff of life."

Application 1 Write sentences that contain fresh substitutes for the clichés listed below.

a. please bear in mind _____

_____

b. a lover of nature and the great outdoors _____

_____

c. The best laid plans of mice and men often go awry. _____

_____

d. red as a beet _____

_____

e. the fact of the matter _____

_____

Application 2 Rewrite the following paragraph so that all exhausted words and phrases are replaced by fresher vocabulary.

America is truly the great melting pot. Since time immemorial, our shores have welcomed the teeming millions of the world who came here seeking life, liberty, and the pursuit of happiness. From all walks of life they came to our great cities. For many, it was no bed of roses. Ghettoes developed and spread like the plague. But the immigrants triumphed despite overwhelming odds. They took the bull by the horns and made the world a better place to live in for their children.

_____

CHAPTER 8

Technical Words:
Jargon

Jargon is the special vocabulary that is used by a professional group. Lawyers, automobile mechanics, psychologists, and English teachers, among others, have their own technical vocabulary. This is "shop talk" that makes sense to them, but not necessarily to those outside the profession. An automobile mechanic would know what *timing* is; an English teacher *pentameter;* a psychologist *autistic.* Any profession that you enter will have jargon associated with it; moreover, you have to master jargon to survive in many college courses.

Hint: When using technical words, always make certain that the average reader will understand them. Provide definitions, details, and illustrations for jargon.

In writing, where you have to consider your audience, you should not use jargon simply to impress the reader with your technical knowledge of a field. Where jargon must be used (for instance, if you were writing a paper on hi-fi equipment you might use words like *monaural, coaxial, distortion, woof,* and *quadraphonic*), take care to inform the reader of special meanings. Never bombard the reader with too much jargon, whether it relates to an academic course, a profession, a hobby, or a sport.

Application.   Select a field (a sport, hobby, or profession) which you know fairly well, and list five specialized words relating to it. Then write a sentence in which you define the word, give details about it, or give concrete illustrations of it. Here is an example:

a. *Squeeze play* (from baseball). Baseball's squeeze play, in which the batter swings at anything in order to "coax" or "squeeze" a runner home from third base, was perfected by Jackie Robinson and his teammates on the old Brooklyn Dodgers.

b. _____
_____
_____

c. _____
_____
_____

d. _____
_____
_____

e. _____
_____
_____

f. _____
_____
_____

CHAPTER 9

Disguised Words: Euphemisms

Modern American speech is filled with *euphemisms*—with words and phrases used as substitutes for vocabulary that might be unpleasant or embarrassing. Euphemisms are words that disguise or camouflage meanings. This is illustrated perfectly by a Jules Feiffer cartoon in which a slum dweller states: "First I was poor. Then I became needy. Then I was underprivileged. Now I'm disadvantaged. I still don't have a penny to my name—but I have a great vocabulary." Reliance on euphemisms might be surprising in light of the "frankness" with which people use language in the 1970's. Yet as a *Time* magazine writer observes, housewives who can talk candidly about their sex lives to their doctors will still tell their children to "go to the potty." Euphemisms obviously have a great deal of social (and also political) utility.

Euphemisms can be employed in misleading and dishonest ways. Thus, in the language of Watergate, an event could be "rendered inoperative," which meant that it never existed. Similarly, "stonewalling" signified the refusal to answer. In advertising, "facial-quality tissue" refers to toilet paper. And in sociology a "culturally deprived environment" is a catchall phrase referring to an impoverished home or learning area. Taken to extremes, euphemistic language (combined frequently with jargon) can be utterly meaningless, as in the phrase "synchronized organizational capability," which certainly sounds impressive but lacks any real significance.

> *Hint:* Do not hide your real meaning behind euphemisms unless you think that the audience might be genuinely offended by a more direct statement.

In writing, it is generally best to assume that readers can deal with unpleasant realities and that you do not have to sugarcoat your vocabulary. In correcting a euphemism, you do not want to lapse into a *vulgarism,* or obscenity, which would happen if you were to substitute various four-letter words for "going to the potty." Fortunately, there is normally a middle range which permits you to be direct without offending your general audience.

Application 1 Give the actual meaning of the following euphemisms.

a. senior citizen _____

b. pacification program _____

c. facial blemish _____

d. dentures _____

e. undesirable elements _____

Application 2 List five euphemisms that you use from time to time and explain why you use them.

a. _____   d. _____

b. _____   e. _____

c. _____

CHAPTER 10

Wordiness

Wordiness is simply the use of too many words to establish your meaning. In speech, we all know what a long-winded person is. In politics, Hubert Humphrey is famous for his "wordy" speeches. Similarly, in television, there is something known as "pie"—words and actions designed to make a show run for the required time but which actually aren't necessary to the plot. However, in writing, where ideas should be presented clearly and forcefully, we have to make all words count.

Hint: Eliminate all words that do not add to the meaning of a sentence— that exist merely as padding for your paper.

Words and expressions that do not count are sometimes termed "dead wood." Such words do not contribute to the ideas that we want to express. Frequently they exist only to permit us to reach the 250- or 500- word count that a teacher requires. But wordiness hurts the focus of your paper and blurs meanings. It is a clear signal to the reader that you do not have enough to say, or that you haven't thought enough about your subject.

Some of the most common forms of wordiness include the following.

1. *Useless words and phrases:*

These add absolutely nothing to the meaning of the sentence and can be eliminated easily.

Wordy   The American flag now has fifty stars in number.
Improved   The American flag has fifty stars.

2. *Padded expressions.*

These often occur in conversation because they permit us to gather our thoughts. In writing, they can be eliminated or reduced to a single word.

Wordy   In my opinion; I think that; it seems to me
Improved (eliminate)
Wordy   due to the fact that
Improved because
Wordy   in a curious manner
Improved curiously
Wordy   the reason why
Improved (eliminate)
Wordy   in many instances
Improved often

3. *Careless repetition of words and ideas.*

When you use the same word, you are risking wordiness and monotony. This is also true when you repeat an idea twice (which we term "redundancy").

Repetition of word The park was dark and gloomy, with gloom-filled trees in a darkening sky.

       Improved The park, with its dark trees and deepening sky, was gloomy.

Repetition of idea Darlene enjoys going to discotheques because they are a delight for her on weekends.

       Improved Darlene enjoys going to discotheques on weekends.

Eliminating wordiness is a main objective in revising your papers (see Chapter 43, pp. 250–251). But even in the first version of your composition, it is best to be economical and direct in your choice of words.

Application 1   Revise the following sentences to eliminate wordiness.

a. We gathered together around the professor, Dr. Davis. ———

———————————————————

b. In spite of the fact that he is considerably over sixty, Sam Snead continues to play good golf today. ——————————

———————————————————

———————————————————

c. San Francisco is rainy and cold in December, as wet and chilly as you can imagine. _____

_____

_____

d. The television program "The Tonight Show" offers to late-night television viewers a program centering on one of television's top celebrities, Johnny Carson. _____

_____

_____

e. Hard work appeals to me in a strange and unusual sort of way.

_____

_____

Application 2   List several useless words or padded expressions that you hear in conversation or use yourself.

a. _____   d. _____

b. _____   e. _____

c. _____   f. _____

CHAPTER 11

Troublesome Words: Sound-Alikes and Look-Alikes

Any word can be troublesome if you don't know it or if you misuse it. However, there are certain pairs and sets of words that are especially troublesome. These are words which resemble each other in sound, and perhaps in spelling, but which have different meanings. We use many of these "sound-alikes" (which are called homonyms) and "look-alikes" in writing. Consequently, we have to distinguish between such words as *affect* and *effect,* or *device* and *devise.* Thirty of the most common sound-alikes and look-alikes appear below.

1. *accept:* to receive or give a positive answer to.
   except: to leave out; reject.
2. *affect:* to influence; to produce an effect upon.
   effect: the result; to accomplish or bring to pass.
3. *already:* previously; by or before the given time.
   all ready: completely prepared.
4. *all together:* in a group.
   altogether: wholly; completely.
5. *allusion:* a reference to something else.
   illusion: an unreal, misleading, or deceptive appearance.
6. *anyone:* any person at all.
   any one: one specific person in a group.
7. *beside:* by the side of; except.
   besides: in addition to; except.
8. *breath:* air taken into and let out of the lungs.
   breathe: to inhale and exhale.
9. *buy:* to purchase
   by: next to; near to; according to.
10. *capital:* primary; major; wealth; a center of government.
    Capitol: the building in which the U.S. Congress meets.

11. *cloth:* a piece of fabric.
    clothe: to cover the body.
12. *complement:* that which completes; a complete set.
    compliment: something said in praise or admiration.
13. *device:* a plan; an invention; a design.
    devise: to plan, invent, think out.
14. *emigrate:* to leave one place in order to live in another.
    immigrate: to come to reside in a country where one is not a native.
15. *formally:* with regard to ceremony, form, arrangement, rules.
    formerly: in the past; some time ago.
16. *hear:* to listen to; consider; become aware of.
    here: at or in this place.
17. *its:* shows ownership.
    it's: a contraction (shortened form) of *it is.*
18. *later:* at a later time; after some time.
    latter: last mentioned of the two; near the end.
19. *lead:* to show the way; a specific metal.
    led: directed; conducted; guided.
20. *loose:* to set free; not fastened; too large.
    lose: to misplace or accidentally leave behind.
21. *passed:* . past tense of the verb *to pass.*
    past: that which has already happened.
22. *peace:* calm; harmony; freedom from disturbance.
    piece: a part of something.
23. *principal:* the chief person or head.
    principle: a rule; right conduct; an essential element.
24. *stationary:* not moving; unchanging.
    stationery: writing materials.
25. *than:* used in a comparison.
    then: refers to time; an action taking place at a certain time.
26. *their:* shows ownership.
    there: indicates a direction.
    they're: a contraction (shortened form) of *they are.*
27. *to:* indicates a direction toward a place or destination.
    too: also; in addition; in excess.
    two: the number 2.
28. *weather:* the general condition of the atmosphere; to wear away.
    whether: if it be the case or fact that; in case that.
29. *who's:* a contraction (shortened form) of *who is.*
    whose: the possessive form of *who.*
30. *your:* the possessive form of *you;* of, belonging to, or done by you.
    you're: a contraction (shortened form) of *you are.*

For a much fuller collection of explanations about words—one that includes look-alikes, sound-alikes, and much more—the following specialized dictionary is recommended: H. W. Fowler, *A Dictionary of Modern English Usage.*

Application 1   Write sentences in which you use the following words correctly.

a. already _____

b. any one _____

c. loose _____

d. then _____

e. who's _____

f. too _____

Application 2   Write definitions for the following sets of words. Consult a dictionary if necessary.

a. respectfully/respectively _____

_____

b. adapt/adopt _____

_____

c. farther/further _____

_____

d. quiet/quite _____

_____

e. bear/bare _____

_____

f. conscious/conscience _____

_____

CHAPTER 12

Successful Spelling

If we spell poorly (and even major writers have been terrible spellers), the easiest way to avoid misspelling is to consult a dictionary—to literally perch it on your lap when writing. Unfortunately, we often resemble the character in this cartoon.

(© 1975 United Feature Syndicate, Inc.).

We can identify with Peppermint Patty, who is trying to spell Cardinal *Richelieu*. When we are not certain about the spelling of a word, we have a tendency to fake it and hope for the best. However, if we are writing a paper for a teacher, filling out a job application, or typing a letter for the boss, we cannot afford misspellings.

12.1. Spelling Rules

There are several common mistakes made in spelling that can be eliminated by learning the following rules. Master these rules exactly, or they may do more harm than good.

1. *Put* i *before* e *except after* c, *or when sounded like* a.

(ie):	achieve, believe, siege, friend, thief
(ei):	receive, receipt, ceiling, perceive, conceive
(a sound):	weight, vein, veil, rein
(major exceptions to rule):	either, neither, weird, height, seize; seizure, leisure, foreign, science, forfeit, sleight, counterfeit

2. *Double the final consonant (any letter in the alphabet except* **a, e, i, o,** *and* **u,** *which are vowels) when the word meets all the following tests:*

1. the suffix (*-ed,-ing,-est,* for example) begins with a vowel
2. the word ends with a vowel followed by a consonant
3. the word is one syllable or has its accent (or voice stress) on the last syllable

Examples: begin + ing = beginning
control + able = controllable
bat + er = batter
commit + ed = committed
excel + ent = excellent
forget + ing = forgetting

Hint: *When a suffix is added to a word ending in a silent* e *(an* e *that is not pronounced), the consonant coming before the* e *is never doubled.*

come + ing = coming
interfer + ed = interfered
shine + ing = shining
write + ing = writing

---

3. *Change a final* y *in a word to an* i *if there is a consonant before the* y—*except when the suffix begins with an* i.

Examples: enemies, busily, pitying, iciness, attorneys, annoying, married, carrying, industries, loveliest
Major exceptions: daily, laid, paid, said

4. *Words ending in silent* e *normally keep the* e *with suffixes beginning with a consonant, but drop the* e *before suffixes beginning with a vowel.*

Examples: hopeless, ninety, writing, spiteful, imaginary, careless, likable, lovely, arrangement, arrival

12.2. Guidelines to Good Spelling

Successful spelling involves more than the memorization of rules. Here are more hints to improve your spelling.

1. New words are easy to learn to spell correctly, but words that you have misspelled for years are far more difficult to correct. Identify your most frequent misspellings, emphasize the part of the word that gives you the most trouble, and study only one word at a time to avoid

confusion. Work on one word every day. Since most of your misspellings are caused by a small number of words, you can expect to improve greatly by following this procedure.

2. Develop a series of tricks or memory aids which will help you to remember the correct spelling of difficult words (for instance, "The principal is your PAL," or "You can't believe a LIE").

3. *Repetition* is a key to accurate spelling. Write a new word, a troublesome word, or a word that you have misspelled ten times.

4. *Proofread* your writing. In other words, reread carefully everything that you write. Many spelling errors are simply careless mistakes that can be caught in a thorough proofreading of your paper.

5. Practice "spelling demons." These are words most frequently misspelled by college students. The following list contains many of the most common spelling demons. Make a special effort to master them.

absence	develop	library	repetition
acceptable	disappearance	loneliness	resemblance
accommodate	disappoint	magazine	restaurant
accidentally	division	mathematics	rhythm
achieve	doubt	medicine	ridiculous
adviser	embarrass	misspelled	sacrifice
agreement	environment	monotonous	safety
already	employees	murmur	science
analysis	equipment	naturally	secretary
anxious	existence	necessary	seize
article	familiar	neighborhood	separate
athletics	February	niece	several
attendance	federal	occasion	significant
believe	foreign	occur	similar
benefited	friend	occurred	sincerity
business	government	omitted	sophomore
calendar	grammar	ordinary	succeed
candidate	guidance	parallel	summary
careful	height	particularly	temperament
conceive	heroes	pastime	tendency
continuous	horrible	peaceable	therefore
college	immediately	peculiar	tragedy
column	independence	prejudice	truly
committed	industrial	pronunciation	undoubtedly
companies	interfere	psychology	until
conscious	jealous	quantity	usually
correspondence	judgment	receive	valuable
decision	justified	recommend	view
definite	knowledge	referred	weird

dependent	language	relieve	wherever
description	leisure	religious	writing

Some Useful Books

Here are some books you might want to borrow or buy if you are interested in becoming a strong speller.

J. N. Hook. *Spelling 1500*. New York: Harcourt Brace, 1967.

Norman Lewis. *Twenty Days to Better Spelling*. New York: Harper & Row, 1953.

Julia McCorble. *Learning to Spell: An Informal Guide for College Students*. Boston: D. C. Heath, 1953.

Joseph Mersand. *Spelling Your Way to Success*. New York: Barron's, 1959.

Harry Shefter. *6 Minutes a Day to Perfect Spelling*. New York: Pocket Books, 1954.

Genevieve Love Smith. *Spelling by Principles: A Programmed Text*. Englewood Cliffs, N.J.: Prentice-Hall, 1966.

Application 1 Fill in the missing letters in the following words with *ie* or *ei*.

dec__ve	ch__f	hankerch__f	bel__ve
rel__ve	sh__ld	gr__f	exper__nce
s__ze	for__gn	fr__ght	sc__nce
shr__k	__ther	w__rd	p__rce
n__ghbor	y__ld	w__ght	sl__ght

Application 2 Spell the following words using the suffixes that are suggested.

hit + ing ———————	use + less ———————
easy + ily ———————	hurry + ing ———————
large + er ———————	beg + ar ———————
recite + al ———————	swim + ing ———————
journey + s ———————	ignore + ance ———————
rob + ery ———————	pity + ful ———————
glory + ous ———————	advise + ment ———————
true + ly ———————	tire + less ———————
perceive + ed ———————	boy + ish ———————
break + age ———————	white + ness ———————
deny + al ———————	sincere + ity ———————

PART 2

THE SENTENCE:
Putting Words Together

The basic vehicle for communication is the sentence. It can consist of single words ("Wait." "Stop!" "Why?"), although such short structures usually occur in speech rather than in writing. On the other hand, hundreds of words can be used to structure a single sentence. (The Nobel prize novelist William Faulkner has sentences running to three or four pages in some of his books.) Regardless of length, there is much that we know about sentences, even if we do not know certain vocabulary or cannot identify grammatically the various parts in them. For instance, Lewis Carroll wrote "nonsense verse" like the following line:

the slithy toves did gyre and gimble in the wabe.

Carroll fabricates vocabulary, but our sense of English word order tells us that "toves" (whatever they are) must be the subject, and "did gyre and gimble" (whatever that is) the action that they engaged in. There is a lot of common sense in the way that we select words and structure sentences. Part 2 of this *Handbook* reviews many of the properties of the sentence that are familiar to you, offers strategies for improving sentences, and provides guidelines for avoiding typical grammatical mistakes.

CHAPTER 13

Parts of Speech

The parts of speech in any language are classes of words that have certain *forms* and *functions* in a sentence. We know that an automobile carburetor has a certain form and function in an engine which distinguishes it from a generator. Similarly, a noun has certain forms (it can change its form through the addition of an *-s* or *-es* which transforms it from singular to plural), but it also functions in several ways in a sentence, typically as the subject of a verb. The main parts of speech in English are nouns, verbs, pronouns, adjectives, adverbs, prepositions, and conjunctions. Just as we have to understand the main components in an engine in order to assemble, disassemble, and fine tune it, we also have to be familiar with parts of speech when working with sentences. This chapter provides a review of the parts of speech. Because these terms appear frequently throughout Part 2, you should master their basic features if you haven't already done so.

13.1. Nouns

A noun is the name of a person, place, thing, quality, concept, or condition.

Person   Pat Brown
Place   Houston
Thing   desk
Quality   simplicity
Concept   wisdom
Condition   nervousness

Proper nouns relate to specific people, places, and things. *Common nouns* relate to any unspecified member of a group.

Hint: Proper nouns are always capitalized. Common nouns are not capitalized unless they are the first word in a sentence.

Most nouns can form a plural or be made a possessive, as demonstrated in the following cases:

singular to plural   one book/two books
forming the possessive   summer's pleasures

Moreover, many suffixes (or word endings) that are added to words produce nouns. These include words ending in -age, -al, -ance, -ant, -ar, -ard, -cation, -cy, -dom, -ee, -ent, -er, -ese, -hood, -ice, -ion, -ism, -ist, -ite, -ity, -ment, -ness, -or, -ry, -ship, -sion, -tion, and -ure.

link + **age**	= linkage
govern + **ance**	= governance
sister + **hood**	= sisterhood
introduce + **tion**	= introduction
high + **ness**	= highness

These are some fundamental qualities concerning the form of a noun. The main functions of nouns will be discussed in subsequent sections.

13.2. Verbs

A verb is a word that expresses action or state of being. It works typically with its subject to create the basic meaning of a sentence.

The quarterback threw an outlet pass.

ACTION

I am sick.

BEING

The form of a verb is easy to detect because most verbs have the following features.

a. a singular present tense form ending in -s or -es

Reggie Jackson hits fastball pitchers well.

b. a regular (-ed) or irregular past tense form

Malcolm X benefited from his trip to Mecca.

c. a present participle (-ing) form

Barnum and Bailey is coming to Atlanta.

d. a past participle form (an unchanging form that can be combined with helping verbs like *has* and *have* to make verbs of more than one word)

Martin had drunk too much wine.

There are six basic tenses in English, represented in the following diagram.

Present   I help
Past   I helped
Future   I will help, I shall help
Present Perfect   I have helped
Past Perfect   I had helped
Future Perfect   I will (shall) have helped

> **Hint:** Use *will* for future and future perfect tenses, except when *shall* is needed to convey the idea of obligation.

These are grammatical functions that should not be treated too simply, because the *idea of time* that each tense conveys can be complicated. For instance, the present tense can actually express the present, the past, the future, or the habitual as action relates to time.

Present Tense–Present Time   She drops the cup.
Present Tense–Past Time   Then he jumps up and comes at me.
Present Tense–Future Time   Marlene returns from Phoenix tomorrow.
Present Tense–Habitual Time   I drive to work every day.

In addition to tense, verbs also have the characteristics of *voice, mood,* and *number. Voice* tells the reader whether the subject of the verb is performing the action of the verb (the *active* voice) or is being acted upon (the *passive* voice).

Active Voice   She takes tranquilizers.
Passive Voice   The batter was struck by the ball.

The passive voice always utilizes some form of the verb *to be* (see p. 68) and a past participle.

> **Hint:** Avoid overreliance on passive constructions because they are weak (the subject does not act, but instead is acted upon) and wordy.

Mood reveals the function of a verb in order to make a statement or command, or to express a desire, doubt, or possibility. The three moods in Modern English are *indicative, subjunctive,* and *imperative.* The indicative mood expresses a fact or what is believed to be a fact, or asks a question:

The massacre at Ponce still angers many Puerto Ricans.
He thinks that teachers receive too much vacation time.
Is Roberta Flack appearing at Carnegie Hall?

The subjunctive mood expresses a condition contrary to fact. It also indicates a wish, doubt, obligation, potentiality, or desirability:

I wish that President Kennedy were still alive.
If American cities were properly funded by Congress, there would be more
    manageable urban problems.
I demanded that he return the money.

The imperative mood makes a command, demand, suggestion, or request:

Stop!
Leave him alone.
Return the book to the library.

Like nouns and pronouns, verbs also have the characteristic of number; in other words, they have singular and plural forms. If a subject is singular in number, the verb will be singular in number. If a subject is plural in number, the verb will be plural in number.

She plays the guitar well.

SINGULAR SINGULAR
SUBJECT   VERB

They enjoy a good game of poker.

PLURAL   PLURAL
SUBJECT   VERB

Verbs are more complicated in form and function than this brief introduction to them suggests. Additional chapters in Part 2 are devoted to the proper use of verbs.

13.3. Pronouns

A pronoun is a word used in place of another noun or pronoun. The word replaced is the *antecedent* of the pronoun. Pronouns have many functions in sentences and can cause numerous problems, but primarily they are used to avoid the needless repetition of persons, places, and things.

The pronouns employed most frequently in writing are called *personal pronouns* and can be singular or plural. Personal pronouns also have *case* (subjective, objective, possessive), which means that they have varying functions in a sentence. Finally, personal pronouns are classified in terms of *gender,* or according to sex. The diagram below illustrates the main features of personal pronouns.

	Subjective	Objective	Possessive
First Person			
Singular	I	me	mine
Plural	we	us	ours
Second Person			
Singular	you	you	yours
Plural	you	you	yours
Third Person			
Singular			
Masculine	he	him	his
Feminine	she	her	hers
Neuter	it	it	its
Any gender	one	one	one's
Plural			
All genders	they	them	theirs

Notice how case illuminates the functions of pronouns in the following sentences.

Subjective Case   *I (We, You, He, She, They)* arrived at the theater late.
Objective Case   The captain dislikes *me (us, you, him, her, it, them).*
Possessive Case   The winning number was *mine (ours, yours, his, hers, theirs).*

There are several other classes of pronouns, including these important groups:

Demonstrative Pronouns (point out persons or things):   *this, that, these, those.*
Indefinite Pronouns (do not take the place of any specific noun):   *all, anybody, anyone, anything, both, each, either, everybody, everyone, everything, few, many, neither, nobody, none, nothing, one, plenty, several, some, somebody, someone.*
Interrogative Pronouns (are used to ask questions):   *who, whom, whose, which, what, whoever, whatever.*
Relative Pronouns (refer to people or places and are used in three cases):

Subjective	Objective	Possessive
who	whom	whose
that	that	of that
which	which, whom	of which, whose

Intensive Pronouns (end in *-self* or *-selves* and used to strengthen the subject of a verb, as in "I went to town myself"): *myself, yourself, himself, herself, ourselves, yourselves, themselves, oneself, itself.*

Reflexive Pronouns (personal pronouns ending in *-self* or *-selves* and used in sentences where the action of a verb is directed toward its subject, as in "She let herself in the apartment"): *myself, yourself, himself, herself, ourselves, yourselves, themselves, oneself, itself.*

Because there are several classes of pronouns, many involving number, case, and gender, they create difficult choices in writing. Several sections in this part of the *Handbook* provide guidelines for the correct application of pronouns.

13.4. Adjectives

An adjective is a word that modifies (describes, limits, or changes the meaning of) a noun or pronoun. It normally tells "how many," "how much," "what kind of," or "which."

How many   Numerous African tribes were destroyed by slave traders.
How much   Five dollars doesn't buy much food anymore.
What kind of   Accurate spelling is required in this class.
Which   The green car is mine.

Most adjectives have three forms—*absolute, comparative,* and *superlative.* In other words, the stem form can be compared with its *-er* (or "more") and *-est* (or "most") forms.

Absolute	*Comparative*	*Superlative*
tall	taller	tallest
easy	easier, more easy	easiest, more easy
beautiful	more beautiful	most beautiful

> **Hint:** For adjectives with three or more syllables, use only the "more" or "most" forms.

Because *adverbs* (see 13.5) also can be compared, it is necessary to distinguish the difference in function between adjectives and adverbs. Adjectives normally come before the nouns or pronouns they modify:

It was a beautiful day.

ADJECTIVE NOUN

It was a clear, bright, and beautiful day.

           ADJECTIVES   NOUN

They can also come after a noun, as in the following patterns:

The day, clear and bright, was perfect.

     NOUN   ADJECTIVES

The Super Bowl in an event so popular that it is sold out months in advance.

          NOUN   ADJECTIVE

A second valuable way to distinguish adjectives in sentences is to look for adjective-forming suffixes: *-able, -al, -an, -ant, -ate, -ative, -ent, -ful, -ic, -ish, -ive, -less, -like, -ory, -ous, -some,* and -y. When these suffixes are added to nouns, they form adjectives.

Noun	*Adjective*
fate	fatal
truth	truthful
break	breakable

Many adjectives come after *verbs of being* (formed from *to be*) or after *verbs of the senses* (relating to seeing, smelling, hearing, feeling, tasting, appearing, or becoming).

Clark Gable was handsome.

     VERB OF BEING   ADJECTIVE

Pizza always smells good.

     VERB OF SENSES   ADJECTIVE

Practically every word that comes after such verbs is an adjective (unless it is a noun).

Finally, there are special types of adjectives that are called *articles* (or *determiners*).

A banana is nourishing.
An orange should be juicy.
The melon is not ripe yet.

> *Hint:* The standard advice to use *a* before a word beginning with a consonant and *an* before a word starting with a vowel is not always correct. Sometimes you must use your ear to determine if the combination of sounds is right.

13.5. Adverbs

An adverb is a word that modifies a verb, an adjective, or another adverb.

ADVERB + VERB
The siren sounded suddenly.

           VERB   ADVERB

ADVERB + ADJECTIVE
Crazy Horse was a very famous Sioux.

        ADVERB ADJECTIVE

ADVERB + ADVERB
Joe Namath throws a football remarkably hard.

        ADVERB ADVERB

Adverbs are usually formed by adding the suffix *-ly* to adjectives *(sudden suddenly; extreme extremely; real really)*. However, the *-ly* suffix does not always create an adverb. Adjectives also have them *(lonely, kingly)*, although not typically. Adverbs ending in *-ly* are called "pure" and can be compared, along with other adverb forms:

Absolute	*Comparative*	*Superlative*
firmly	more firmly	most firmly
fast	faster	fastest

Some common adverbs, normally modifying verbs, do not have *-ly* endings:

after	never	then
always	now	there
before	often	too
here	quite	seldom
not	soon	very

The number of important adverbs in this category is relatively small; thus you should not drop the -*ly* from adverbs indiscriminately. In colloquial speech and dialect, the tendency to drop the -*ly* from the following common adverbs is quite usual:

badly	quietly
considerably	really
differently	seriously
nearly	surely
neatly	terribly

Colloquial   It hurt considerable.
Written   It hurt considerably.

Occasionally you will encounter adverbs that have both pure and "flat" (without the -*ly*) forms which can be used interchangeably. Words like *cheap, deep, loud, rough, sharp, slow,* and *wrong* are in this category. Thus it would be equally correct to say "Don't run so slow" and "Don't run so slowly."

From the examples of adverbs provided in this section, it should be apparent that adverbs tend to fall into several major classes: adverbs of time *(early, late, recently, soon);* adverbs of place *(upstairs, south, here, there);* adverbs of manner *(nicely, poorly, well);* and adverbs of degree *(very, rather, extremely).* Recognition of these functions will help you to locate adverbs in writing.

13.6. Prepositions

A preposition is a word that expresses a specific relationship. It is a connective that shows the relationship between two words and that carries the sense of time, position, direction, or another concept. ("There are many women *in* the class who work, maintain families, and also attend college.") A phrase introduced by a preposition—"in the class"—is a *prepositional phrase* (see p. 94). Always choose the right preposition to convey the precise relationship between words.

Here is a list of the most commonly used simple and compound prepositions:

about	away from	in back of	out of
above	beneath	in case of	outside
across	beside	in front of	owing to
after	besides	in light of	through
against	between	in place of	throughout
ahead of	beyond	inside	till

along	but	inside of	to
amid	by	instead of	together with
among	by means of	into	toward
apart from	by way of	in view of	towards
around	concerning	like	under
as far as	contrary to	near	until
as for	despite	of	up
aside from	due to	off	up at
as to	during	on	up on
as well as	in	on account of	upon
at	in addition to	out	up to

Choosing the correct preposition can be difficult at times, especially for people who are not native speakers of English and for those who speak the dialect of a particular area. Several main areas of proper preposition usage are outlined later in this *Handbook* (see pp. 104 to 108).

13.7. Conjunctions

Conjunctions are words that are used to link words and groups of words known as phrases and clauses (see pp. 92 to 95). Along with pronouns, determiners, and prepositions, they are *structure words* that help us to assemble the other parts of speech (nouns, verbs, adjectives, and adverbs) in a sentence.

Conjunctions are divided into three classes—*coordinating* conjunctions, *subordinating* conjunctions, and *correlative* conjunctions. Coordinating conjunctions join words and word groups of equal rank and importance. The five coordinating conjunctions are *and, or, but, for,* and *nor.*

Hint: Coordinating conjunctions signify the following qualities:
  and = adding together
  or = choice
  but = opposition
  for = reason
  nor = opposition

Subordinating conjunctions join less important, dependent clauses to main, independent clauses in a sentence. Some key subordinating conjunctions are *after, although, as, as if, because, before, if, no matter how, now that, once, provided that, since, so, so that, though, unless, when, whenever, while,* and *whereas.*

Correlative conjunctions join pairs. (A correlative is technically a coordinating conjunction.) The five most frequently utilized correlative conjunctions are *both . . . and, either . . . or, neither . . . nor, not only . . . but also,* and *whether . . . or.*

Application 1 Write a noun for each noun-forming suffix listed.

a. -age —————————— f. -ness——————————

b. -ard —————————— g. -or ——————————

c. -cation —————————— h. -ry ——————————

d. -ion —————————— i. -ship ——————————

e. -ment —————————— j. -tion ——————————

Application 2 Diagram the six basic tenses for the verb *to figure* in the first person *(I).*

Present ————————————————————————

Past ——————————————————————————

Future —————————————————————————

Present Perfect ———————————————————————

Past Perfect ————————————————————————

Future Perfect ———————————————————————

Application 3 Give the mood (imperative, subjunctive, or indicative) of the italicized verbs below.

a. *Give* it to me immediately! ——————————

b. I wish that I *were* rich. ——————————

c. Florida already *suffers* from a population explosion. ——————————

d. Booker T. Washington *represents* a conservative tendency in modern black thought. ——————————

e. *Watch* out for reckless drivers. ——————————

f. Let it not *be said* that this rich nation cannot feed its poor. ————————

Application 4 Supply appropriate pronouns for the following sentences.

a. The car, _____ has a good engine, is reasonably priced.

b. _____ can pass Professor Davidson's course.

c. _____ enjoyed _____ trip to Arizona.

d. _____ dirty laundry is piled in the closet?

e. Governor Brown rarely permits _____ a moment of luxury.

f. Give me _____ pen.

g. Cesar Chavez _____ was in town.

h. Flip Wilson, _____ used to have a weekly show, now only does television specials.

Application 5   Make adjectives for the adjective-forming suffixes listed.

a. -able _____   f. -ful _____

b. -al _____   g. -ic _____

c. -an _____   h. -ish _____

d. -ate _____   i. -ive _____

e. -ent _____   j. -some _____

Application 6   Use an adverb of time, manner, place, and degree in these sentences.

a. He was _____ for work.   (time)

b. Dick does housework _____   (manner)

c. We traveled _____ to enjoy the sun.   (place)

d. The dogs have _____ ruined the front yard.   (degree)

Application 7   Underline all prepositions in the following sentences.

a. I am going to San Juan for a vacation.

b. It is hard for a camel to pass through the eye of a needle.

c. Keep away from the expressway on rainy days.

d. After the concert we went to a restaurant for hamburgers and beer.

e. He rushed to put money in the meter during an intermission in the program.

Application 8   Supply appropriate conjunctions for the sentences in this exercise.

a. Mary Ann started for Denise's house, _____ she never got there.

b. _____ the university budget has been reduced, students and faculty have not lost hope.

c. The result of voter indifference is weak representation, _____ the result of weak representation is bad government.

d. Not only has the United States been hurt by inflation, _____ the nation has been damaged by recession.

e. The college refused to invite the historian, _____ he was a communist.

CHAPTER 14

Understanding the Sentence

As a basic definition, we can say that a sentence is *a group of words that expresses a complete thought and ends with a period, question mark, or exclamation point.* Sentences in speech can vary considerably in vocabulary and grammar from written sentences. Look, for instance, at the following sentences:

Hey, youngblood, what you think you doin'?
You ain't got a prayer in the world.
He's football player.
It is hard for the family to survive in crowded urban areas.

All these sentences could be (and are) spoken in America today. Yet only one—the last—is the sort of sentence that we encounter in writing and in formal situations. The first sentence represents spoken Black English; the second represents a familiar colloquial construction; and the third represents "Spanglish," or Spanish dialect. Such sentences have their own structural properties that many people employ conversationally in this country. The American language would be impoverished without the many varieties of sentence usage that have emerged from communities, songs, folk sayings, and television programs and films. Archie Bunker, Chico, and George Jefferson, viewed by millions of Americans every week, testify to the richness of the spoken English sentence in the United States.

Written English and standard conversational English also have their color and utility. To a large extent, our social, economic, and vocational mobility and success depend on our ability to master written English, and especially the standard English sentence. If we appear for a job interview, we would not want to use "street" language, or even say, "It doesn't make any difference the salary." Many varieties of spoken English should not appear in college writing unless employed to flavor an essay in strategic places. Writing—and the sentence as the basic unit of writing—should be patterned after the material that you read in newspapers and magazines. This type of writing will permit you to reach a broad audience in an effective way.

14.1. The Complete Sentence

Every complete sentence must have a *simple subject* and *simple predicate*. The simple subject names a person, place, thing, or concept and consists of one word or a group of words. The simple predicate is a verb whose action is complete; in other words, the verb must describe the action or state of being of the subject.

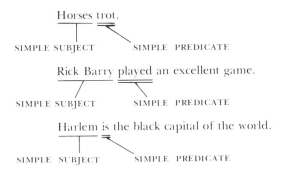

In looking for the subject of a sentence, it is valuable to ask "who" or "what" is performing the action. *What* trots? *Who* played an excellent game? *What* is the black capital of the world?

In most sentences (like those above), the subject comes before the verb. Here are additional guidelines for locating subjects:

1. **When you make a command or a strong statement, the subject will be hidden. In other words, the subject, which is always "you," is not written.**

(You) Stop!
(You) Write to me immediately.

2. **When you form questions, the subject usually comes after the verb or is surrounded by the verb.**

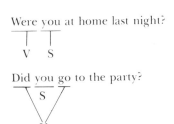

3. *In sentences beginning with* **There,** *the subject will come after the verb.*

There is a good restaurant nearby.

V   S

There are two people in the lobby.

V   S

4. *Some sentences have more than one subject for the same verb.*

Boston and San Francisco have relatively low crime rates.

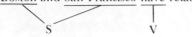
S   V

The Supremes and the Jackson Five are my favorite singing groups.

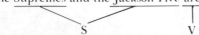
S   V

A simple subject-verb pattern is modified typically by the addition of an *object* that receives the action of the verb. A *direct object* is a noun or pronoun that receives the action of a *transitive* verb. (A transitive verb transfers action to a direct object, as distinguished from an *intransitive* verb, which does not have a direct object.)

Cleon lost his history book.

S   V   DO

Direct objects answer the question "what" or "who" is receiving the action of the verb. *What* was lost?

An *indirect* object is a word or group of words that receive the direct object. It appears commonly between a verb and a direct object, or after a direct object.

J. C. Penney mailed the bill to me.

S   V   DO   IO

J. C. Penney mailed me the bill.

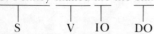
S   V   IO   DO

Indirect objects ask "to whom" or "for whom" is something done. *To whom* did J. C. Penney mail the bill?

Another basic way to extend the subject-verb element in a sentence is through the addition of a *complement*. The complement is a word or group of words that complete the meaning of a *linking* verb (a verb that expresses being, feeling, and seeming).

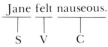

Note here that no action is being reported—simply a condition. The verb links *Jane* with *nauseous,* which is the complement of *felt.* Complements usually occupy the position of objects in a sentence.

14.2. Sentence Types

We do not, or should not, write strings of simple sentences like the ones used so far as examples. A *simple sentence* has only one subject-verb core. On the other hand, a *compound sentence* has two subject-verb cores, each expressing a complete thought and joined by a coordinating conjunction (or a semicolon):

Here it is worth noting that these two independent thoughts could be separate sentences; actually they are *independent clauses,* or units possessing a subject and active verb inserted into the total structure of the sentence.

A third type of sentence is the *complex sentence,* in which a complete independent clause is supported by one or more *dependent* clauses. The dependent clause is the less important idea, or subordinate part, which is not a complete sentence and cannot stand by itself. The dependent clause is signaled by a subordinating conjunction, a relative pronoun, or certain adverbs indicating time, place, and manner.

Because you have excellent grades,

SUBORDINATING   DEPENDENT CLAUSE
CONJUNCTION

   you probably will receive a full-tuition fellowship.

       INDEPENDENT CLAUSE

The road that winds along the California coast is beautiful.

     RELATIVE   DEPENDENT CLAUSE
     PRONOUN
       INDEPENDENT CLAUSE

Whenever there is an increase in the crime rate,

ADVERB   DEPENDENT CLAUSE

citizens demand increased police protection.

INDEPENDENT CLAUSE

Complex sentences are valuable because they permit us to establish the relative importance of units and ideas in a sentence.

Compound-complex sentences are a fourth type that incorporate two or more main clauses and one or more subordinate clauses. These sentences tend to be somewhat awkward in writing, and consequently they should be used sparingly. Compound-complex sentences take many forms. Here is an example:

The courses are enjoyable, and I can work in

INDEPENDENT CLAUSE   INDEPENDENT

the afternoon if I budget my time properly.

CLAUSE   DEPENDENT CLAUSE

An ability to employ all sentence types in writing gives you flexibility and a means of varying and emphasizing your material.

14.3. Modifiers

All words in a sentence that are not subjects, verbs, direct objects, indirect objects, or complements are called *modifiers*. The function of a modifier is to limit, define, identify, or make more exact the meaning of the five main sentence elements. Modifiers can consist of a single word or of groups of words forming clauses and phrases. (A *phrase* is a group of words that does not contain a subject or verb.)

Fidel Castro talked furiously.

(The verb *talked* is made more precise by the modifier *furiously.*)

The house by the station is old.

(The subject *house* is modified by the phrase *by the station.*)

The guitarist played a bright, cheerful tune.

(The direct object *tune* is modified by *bright, cheerful.*)

It is important to know something about modifiers because they contribute to the texture and meaning of sentences. They especially permit enormous flexibility with simple sentences, which do not have to express simple ideas.

Application 1   Supply subjects for the following predicates.

a. _____ hit the ball hard.

b. _____ exists.

c. Where does the _____ end?

d. The _____ spoke of her progressive voting record.

e. _____ stems from labor's reluctance to be more militant.

Application 2   Complete the following sentences with objects.

a. Jim baked _____.

b. Malcolm X died _____.

c. Police are ticketing _____.

d. The store reduced _____.

e. Some local toughs ruined _____.

Application 3   Expand the three sentences below to at least fifteen words each.

a. Dogs bite. _____

_____

b. Our candidate lost. _____

_____

c. The wrong meal arrived. _____

_____

Application 4   Look in a newspaper, magazine, or book and find an example of a simple sentence, a compound sentence, a complex sentence, and a compound-complex sentence. Write an example of each of these kinds of sentences in the space provided and be prepared to analyze them in class.

a. simple sentence _____

_____

b. compound sentence _____

_____

c. complex sentence _____

_____

d. compound-complex sentence _____

_____

_____

CHAPTER 15

Verb Forms

Verbs expressing action or being, which are needed in a complete sentence, tell what is happening and when it is happening. Verbs change their form more than any other part of speech. This is why they cause so many problems in writing.

A verb has four main parts (called a *paradigm*) from which all tenses are derived. Here is how the paradigm looks for the verb *visit:*

Infinitive Form	to visit	(*to* plus verb)
Present	visit	(drops *to* from infinitive)
Past	visited	(add *-ed* or *-d*)
Past Participle	visited	(always used with an auxilliary or "helping" verb like *has, have, had, will have, shall have*)

The following chart on page 66 shows the paradigm at work for a *regular* verb, which is a verb that adds *-ed* or *-d* to form the past tense and past participle.

Certain dialects, and notably Black English, make several significant changes in the features of regular verbs. In fact, the verb structure in dialect is a key element in distinguishing it from written English. Here are two major comparative points.

1. In Black English and several other dialects the *-s* or *-es* suffix is not used to identify the third person singular verbs in the present tense.

Dialect Jerry play ball.
Written Jerry plays ball.

2. The *-ed* suffix that makes the past tense and past participle forms does not appear in black and Hispanic dialects.

Dialect She walk to work yesterday.
Written She walked to work yesterday.

Hint: Do not omit the required *-e* or *-es* from third person singular verbs in the present tense or the *-ed* from past tense and past participle forms.

REGULAR VERB CHART

TO HELP
(the infinitive form)

	Present (stem form = help)	Past (stem form + -ed or -d)	Past participle (stem form + -ed or -d + a helping verb)
	Present tense	**Past tense**	**Present perfect tense**
1st person	I help	I helped	I have helped
2nd person	you help	you helped	you have helped
3rd person	he, she, it helps	he, she, it helped	he, she, it has helped
	we help	we helped	we have helped
	you help	you helped	you have helped
	they help	they helped	they have helped
	Future tense		**Past perfect tense**
1st person	I will help		I had helped
2nd person	you will help		you had helped
3rd person	he, she, it will help		he, she, it had helped
	we will help		we had helped
	you will help		you had helped
	they will help		they had helped
			Future perfect tense
1st person			I will have helped
			we will have helped
2nd person			you will have helped
			you will have helped
3rd person			he, she, it will have helped
			they will have helped

15.1. Irregular Verb Forms

The verb chart on page 66 can be used for all regular verbs. However, there are more than 200 verb forms that do not fit this pattern. They are called *irregular verbs*. Because many of these irregular verbs are important, you must learn (literally memorize) how they change. Here is a simple classification of irregular verbs that you should use for reference.

IRREGULAR VERBS
WITH THE SAME PRESENT, PAST, AND PAST PARTICIPLE

bet, bet, bet	let, let, let	split, split, split
bid, bid, bid ("offer")	put, put, put	spread, spread, spread
burst, burst, burst	quit, quit, quit	thrust, thrust, thrust
cast, cast, cast	read, read, read	wed, wed, wed
cost, cost, cost	rid, rid, rid	wet, wet, wet
cut, cut, cut	set, set, set	
hit, hit, hit	shed, shed, shed	
hurt, hurt, hurt	spit, spit, spit	

IRREGULAR VERBS
WITH THE SAME PAST AND PAST PARTICIPLE

bend, bent, bent	leave, left, left
bind, bound, bound	lend, lent, lent
bring, brought, brought	light, lighted/lit, lighted/lit
build, built, built	lose, lost, lost
buy, bought, bought,	make, made, made
catch, caught, caught	mean, meant, meant
cling, clung, clung	pay, paid, paid
creep, crept, crept	prove, proved, proved
dig, dug, dug	raise, raised, raised
drag, dragged, dragged	say, said, said
drown, drowned, drowned	seek, sought, sought
feed, fed, fed	shine, shone, shone ("glow")
fight, fought, fought	shine, shined, shined ("polish")
find, found, found	sit, sat, sat
flee, fled, fled	sling, slung, slung
fling, flung, flung	spend, spent, spent
get, got, got (or gotten)	spin, spun, spun
hang, hung, hung ("suspend")	strike, struck, struck
hang, hanged, hanged ("execute")	swing, swung, swung
hold, held, held	teach, taught, taught
keep, kept, kept	think, thought, thought
lay, laid, laid	wring, wrung, wrung
lead, led, led	

IRREGULAR VERBS
WHOSE THREE FORMS
ARE DIFFERENT

am, was, been

arise, arose, arisen

awake, awoke, awaked

bear, bore, borne

begin, began, begun

bid, bade, bidden ("command")

bite, bit, bitten

blow, blew, blown

break, broke, broken

choose, chose, chosen

do, did, done

draw, drew, drawn

drink, drank, drunk

drive, drove, driven

eat, ate, eaten

fall, fell, fallen

fly, flew, flown

forbid, forbade, forbidden

forget, forgot, forgotten

forsake, forsook, forsaken

freeze, froze, frozen

give, gave, given

go, went, gone

grow, grew, grown

hide, hid, hidden

know, knew, known

lie, lay, lain

ride, rode, ridden

ring, rang, rung

rise, rose, risen

see, saw, seen

shake, shook, shaken

show, showed, shown

shrink, shrank, shrunk

slay, slew, slain

speak, spoke, spoken

spring, sprang, sprung

steal, stole, stolen

stink, stank, stunk

strive, strove, striven

swear, swore, sworn

swim, swam, swum

take, took, taken

tear, tore, torn

throw, threw, thrown

wake, woke, waked

wear, woke, waked

write, wrote, written

15.2. The Verb *Be*

The most commonly used verb in English is *be*. This is because it can be used as a helping verb with all other verbs. The verb *be* changes in many ways. Therefore, as with all irregular verbs, you should familiarize yourself with its patterns.

BE
(IRREGULAR VERB)

SINGULAR	PLURAL	SINGULAR	PLURAL
Present tense		*Present perfect tense*	
I am	we are	I have been	we have been
your are	you are	you have been	you have been
he, she, it is	they are	he has been	they have been
Past tense		*Past perfect tense*	
I was	we were	I had been	we had been
you were	you were	you had been	you had been
he was	they were	he had been	they had been
Future tense		*Future perfect tense*	
I will (shall) be	we will (shall) be	I will (shall) have been	we will (shall) have been
you will be	you will be	you will have been	you will have been
he will be	they will be	he will have been	they will have been

One of the most common colloquial and dialect words—*ain't*—derives from *be*. It is the spoken equivilent of *isn't (is not)* or *aren't (are not)* and should not be used in writing or in formal speech.

15.3. Progressive Tenses

The progressive tense expresses degrees of present and past time. It captures an action that exists in the continuing present (the *present progressive*) or an action that was in progress at a specific time in the past (the *past progressive*).

Congress is weakening the Presidency.

PRESENT PROGRESSIVE

Geraldo Rivera was explaining the abuses in mental health care.

PAST PROGRESSIVE

These examples show that progressive tenses are formed by combining some form of the helping verb *be* and an *-ing* completer verb.

> *Hint:* The present progressive verb *is coming* shows future time. *Example:* "Rain is coming to San Francisco tomorrow."

You can avoid misusing the progressive tenses by remembering always to employ a form of *be* with the *-ing* word. The *-ing* verb by itself is not finite, which means that it cannot be used as a predicate in a sentence.

Spoken   James always talking in class.
Written   James is always talking in class.

The example above indicates that the dropping of a linking verb *(is)* is a standard feature of several dialects. In writing, the dropping of the linking verb causes a *sentence fragment* (see pp. 83–87).

15.4. Troublesome Verb Choices

Some pairs and sets of verbs are frequently confused. Here are several troublesome verbs along with guidelines for their correct use.

1. Got *and* have

Certain dialects use the verb *got* instead of *has*.

Dialect (also colloquial)   I got a new suit.
Written   I have a new suit.

or

I have got a new suit.

2. Do, did, *and* done

Spoken forms of the verb *do* vary from written forms.

Spoken   I done the job quickly.
Written   I did the job quickly.

Because *do* is an especially troublesome verb, the following outline might aid you in mastering its forms.

Present	I, we, you, they *do*
	he, she, it *does*
Past	I, you, he, she, it, they *did*
Past Participle	I, you, we, they *have* (had) *done*
	he, she, it *has* (had) done

3. Lie *and* lay

Lie means "to rest" or "recline." Its main parts are *lie, lay, lain.* The *-ing* form of lie is *lying*.

Lie   Let's lie on the sand for an hour or so.
Lay   Yesterday I lay on the sand all afternoon.
Lain   Have you ever lain on the sand too long?
Lying   She was lying on the sand and got a bad sunburn.

Lay means "to put" or "to place." Its main parts are *lay, laid, laid*. The *-ing* form of *lay* is *laying*.

lay[1]   Lay the books on the table.
laid   He laid the groceries on the counter.
laid   The park has been laid out nicely.
laying   They will be laying the foundation next week.

4. sit *and* set

Sit means "to occupy or take a seat." Its main parts are *sit, sat, sat*.

sit   Sit in that chair.
sat   He sat on the bench by the sidelines.
sat   He has sat there for a long time.

Set means "to put" or "to place." Its main parts are *set, set, set*.

set   Let's set the table quickly.
set   She set the coffee on the table.
set   He was certain that he had set the clock for seven o'clock.

5. rise *and* raise

Rise means "to get up" or "to go up." Its main parts are *rise, rose, risen*.

rise(s)   The F-14 jet rises very quickly.
rose   The sun rose at 6:35 this morning.
risen   My uncle has risen very early all his life.

Raise means "to cause something to go up." Its main parts are *raise, raised, raised*.

raise   Raise the window higher.
raised   Several students raised their hands at the same time.
raised   By his actions, the President had raised the danger of war.

6. let *and* leave

Let means "to permit" or "allow." Its main parts are *let, let, let*.

let   Let me go to the pizza parlor.
let   She let the dog roam free.
let   If the police had let the demonstrators march, the riot could have been avoided.

Leave means "to go away from" or "allow to stay." Its main parts are *leave, left, left*.

leave(s)   The train leaves in ten minutes.
left   He left his watch in the washroom.
left   A lost child has been left at the lifeguard station.

---

[1] Note: The past tense of *to lie* and the present tense of *to lay* are the same *(lay)*.

7. can *and* may

Can means "to be able to." It asks whether or not you are able to do something.

Can you ride a horse?
I can play tennis very well.

May means "to have permission to." It asks whether or not you will have permission to do something.

May we go to the rock concert?
You may go to the rock concert if you finish your term paper beforehand.

Application 1 On a separate sheet of paper, construct a verb chart similar to the one on page 68 for one of the following regular verbs: *walk, finish, use, live, love.*

Application 2 Supply the correct form of the irregular verb in the sentences below.

a. Yesterday I _____ across the river.   (swim)

b. Recently robbers _____ into the house across the street. (break)

c. The writing center has_____us many useful things.   (teach)

d. Jean has not _____ much this past year.   (grow)

e. He_____ _____ that inflation would be 12 percent by the end of the year.   (read)

f. The submarine _____ from the ocean floor.   (rise)

g. The photographer _____ toward the motionless deer. (creep)

Application 3 Change the following sentences from varieties of spoken English to conventional written English. Pay special attention to the verb forms.

a. Oliver going to Memphis for the weekend.

_____

b. Diane work hard and look forward to the weekend.

_____

c. I got a problem with my bike.

_____

d. James certainly do like Caroline.

_____

e. There ain't no reason to eliminate the addiction program.

_____

f. I learn a lot at the conference on cooperative education last month.

_____

g. I should of called my wife sooner.

_____

Application 4   Use correct verb forms in the paragraph below.

Ships _____ (enter) New York Harbor for more than four centuries. They _____ (lie) beneath the water today, _____ _____ (bury) in sand and mud. Perhaps there _____ (be) treasure in these ships, but their primary value _____ (be) as a record of commercial life in New York. There _____ (be) numerous nations intimately _____ (engage) in the life of New York. Before long, archeologists _____ (get) into diving gear and begin _____ (explore) the remains of sunken ships that already _____ (detect). It should _____ (prove) _____ (be) a remarkable adventure, _____ (fill) with dangers, yet _____ (promise) some genuine rewards.

CHAPTER 16

Subject and Verb Agreement

A singular subject refers to one person or thing and must be followed by a singular verb. A plural subject refers to two or more persons or things and needs a plural verb. We term this relationship between the subject and the verb *agreement;* in other words, a verb must agree with its subject in person and number. This relationship can be diagramed in the following manner:

SINGULAR SUBJECT + SINGULAR VERB

PLURAL SUBJECT + PLURAL VERB

Notice how the verb matches—or agrees with—the subject in the following sentences:

Occupational therapy is a good subject to major in.

    SINGULAR SUBJECT   SINGULAR VERB

There are more and more adults returning to college today.

    PLURAL VERB   PLURAL SUBJECT

Claudine and Robert think that they will run for student council.

    PLURAL SUBJECT   PLURAL VERB

> *Hint:* Remember that the only time you can add an *-s* or *-es* to a present tense verb is when the subject is singular.

Normally the subject of a sentence is a noun, which can be identified easily as singular or plural by the fact that most nouns ending in *-s* are plural. In both rural and urban dialects, and specifically in Black English, there is sometimes the tendency to omit the *-s* or *-es* from plural nouns. This results in sentences like

The other teacher yell at me.

when the speaker wants to indicate that more than one teacher is yelling at him. In conventional written English, the *-s* is always retained.

A few common nouns do not form their plurals through the addition of an *-s*.

Singular	*Plural*
man	men
woman	women
child	children
tooth	teeth
goose	geese
mouse	mice
foot	feet
crisis	crises
criterion	criteria

Dialect forms again contrast with conventional written forms. In some dialects, *foot* might become *foots*, or *women womens*. Moreover, there is a small number of nouns that do not change from singular to plural: *sheep*, *fish, deer*, and *moose* are among them.

A final way to distinguish between singular and plural nouns is by looking at the *determiners*, or signal words, that come before them

DETERMINER
a
an
each   + SINGULAR NOUNS
every

DETERMINER
all
both
few
many   + PLURAL NOUNS
most
several
some

In summary, it is clear that a basic understanding of the singular and plural forms of nouns and verbs (primarily in the present tense) prevents problems in subject-verb agreement. The guidelines below provide a

review of some noun and verb forms as well as advice about how to solve
more complicated problems in agreement.

**1. *Singular subjects normally do not end in -s and go with singular verbs
which do end in -s.***

The paraprofessional [student] works hard.
no /s = | s =
SINGULAR   SINGULAR
SUBJECT   VERB

**2. *Plural subjects normally do end in −s and go with plural verbs which
do not end in −s.***

Paraprofessional [students] work hard.
| s =   no | s =
PLURAL   PLURAL
SUBJECT   VERB

**3. *A compound subject (a subject composed of two or more nouns or
pronouns) that is joined by* and *is plural and requires a plural verb.***

The American League and National League have slightly different regulations.
PLURAL SUBJECT   PLURAL
                                     VERB/no s

"The Rookies," "Mod Squad," and "Adam-12" glamorize the role of the cop in
                 PLURAL   PLURAL
                 SUBJECT   VERB/no s

America.

**4. *When the following words join the subjects, the verb agrees with the
subject that stands closest to the verb.***

either . . . or
neither . . . nor
nor
not only . . . but also
or

Either Billy the Kid or Wyatt Earp serves as a good example of the glorified

SINGULAR SUBJECT   SINGULAR SINGULAR
SUBJECT   VERB
CLOSEST (s)
TO VERB

Western gunfighter.

Not only the conservative labor leader George Meany, but also American Socialists

PLURAL SUBJECT
CLOSEST TO
VERB

believe in the supremacy of the working class.

PLURAL
VERB
(no s)

5. Words that come between a subject and verb do not change the number of the subject.

The men and women who work in the computer room of the Chase Manhattan

PLURAL SUBJECT

Bank are the only ones who dress casually.

PLURAL
VERB

Poverty, a major problem in this country, has been caused by an improper dis-

SINGULAR SUBJECT   SINGULAR VERB

tribution of wealth.

6. Certain verb phrases come at the start of a sentence and introduce the subject which follows. Those phrases are singular and should be followed by a singular subject.

There is   Here is   Where is

There was   Here was   Where was

There is a bad pothole in the street.

SINGULAR   SINGULAR
VERB   SUBJECT

Here was a clear example of Soviet aggression.

SINGULAR   SINGULAR
VERB   SUBJECT

Where is a good Chinese restaurant?

SINGULAR   SINGULAR
VERB   SUBJECT

These verb phrases are plural and should be followed by a plural subject.

There are   Here are   Where are

There were   Here were   Where were

There are bad potholes in the street.

PLURAL   PLURAL
VERB   SUBJECT

Here are clear examples of American aggression.

PLURAL   PLURAL
VERB   SUBJECT

Where are the best restaurants in town?

PLURAL   PLURAL
VERB   SUBJECT

7. *Words describing an amount (time, money, height, weight, length) frequently look plural but are usually singular and take a singular verb.*

Two weeks is the normal check-out time for a library book.

SINGULAR SINGULAR
SUBJECT   VERB

Four ounces of any antibiotic is normally enough for a child's infection.

SINGULAR   SINGULAR
SUBJECT   VERB

8. *Some subjects seem plural but are singular in meaning and take a singular verb.*

civics	mathematics	news	measles
economics	physics	ethics	mumps

The news on Channel 5 is rarely pleasant.

SINGULAR   SINGULAR
SUBJECT   VERB

Because of vaccination, measles is no longer common among children.

SINGULAR SINGULAR
SUBJECT   VERB

9. Titles of books, newspapers, and films, even though plural in form, take singular verbs.

The Daily News has the largest circulation in New York.

SINGULAR   SINGULAR
SUBJECT   VERB

The Guns of Navarone is a classic war novel.

SINGULAR   SINGULAR
SUBJECT   VERB

The Grapes of Wrath portrays life during the Depression better than any other

SINGULAR   SINGULAR
SUBJECT   VERB

novel of the period.

10. The following introductions to expressions do not change the number of the subject:

in addition to   as well as   together with

including   except   along with

India, as well as parts of Africa, is suffering from widespread famine.

SINGULAR   SINGULAR
SUBJECT   VERB

The United States, together with China and the Soviet Union, has contributed to

SINGULAR SUBJECT   SINGULAR VERB

the bloodshed in Indochina.

11. *The following words usually take a plural verb:*

eyeglasses   riches   thanks

means   scissors   trousers

The trousers were ruined by the dry cleaner.

    PLURAL   PLURAL
    SUBJECT   VERB

The Shah of Iran's riches are beyond calculation.

        PLURAL   PLURAL
        SUBJECT   VERB

12. *Collective subjects (such as* **class, family group, number***) take a singular verb when the subject is treated as a unit. A plural verb is used when the subject refers to individuals of a group.*

The class is studying ecology in Golden Gate Park.

(the   SINGULAR
entire   VERB
class)

The commune are going their separate ways.

(various   PLURAL
members   VERB
of the
commune)

Application 1 Complete the sentences below, making certain that the verb agrees with the subject.

a. Overeating in America _____

b. Not only alcoholism, but also cigarrete smoking _____

_____

c. Joe Namath, Catfish Hunter, and Abdul Jabbar _____

_____

d. The broken eyeglasses _____

e. Twelve months_____

f. The Chicanos in California _____

g. Child abuse, one of many mounting problems in this country, ——

_____

h. There were _____

i. Although physics _____

j. Martin Luther King, along with Malcolm X, _____

_____

k. The Los Angeles Times _____

l. The entire group _____

Application 2   Rewrite the following sentences, changing the subject from singular to plural; then make the verb agree with the new plural subject.

a. This drug makes you talk uncontrollably.

_____

b. For many years man has experimented with various forms of religion.

_____

c. Today's American votes independently.

_____

d. Today, a person has different views on marriage.

_____

Application 3   In the following paragraph change all verbs in the past tense to the present tense.

Summer was the best time of year. The Good Humor man returned to his favorite corner, and children played close to his truck. People came out and sat on the stoops of apartment buildings. The retired teacher, Mrs. Banks, sunned herself in a chair that she placed on the sidewalk. Shops stayed open late, and the smell from the Italian bakery lingered until we were asleep. In summer, the streets lived with the colors and events that we loved best.

_____

_____

Agr

CHAPTER 17

Fixing Sentence Fragments

If you do not have a subject, verb, and complete thought in a word group, you do not have a sentence. These are the minimal requirements of a conventional sentence. A word group that lacks any of these items is called a *sentence fragment*. We use sentence fragments from time to time in speech ("All the way"), and professional writers often utilize fragments (which they term "leaners") in a skillful manner. In normal writing, however, sentence fragments are unacceptable. You must learn to recognize the sentence fragment and correct it if it appears in your writing.

17.1. Fragments Without Subject and Verb

Fragments that lack both a subject and a verb are caused by a tendency (more common in speech than in writing) to let a phrase stand by itself.

Fragment   By a car.

Correction   Andy was hit by a car.

          S   V

In conversation, we can imagine being asked, "How was Andy injured?" and replying, "By a car." However, this is not acceptable in writing, where sentences require a subject and predicate verb.

Many *transitional* phrases and expressions (word groups that serve as a bridge from one sentence to another) also lack subjects and verbs:

Last but not least.

Almost but not quite.

Such phrases rarely contribute to the meaning of a group of sentences and should be eliminated.

There are also countless expressions that carry some meaning, but which do not have a subject and predicate:

To be oppressed.

Without any conviction.

Such contructions have to be expanded in order to function as complete sentences.

17.2. Fragments Without Verbs

A fragment caused by the absence of a verb can occur when the presence of a compound subject and various predicate completers causes a construction to look like a sentence because of its length.

A Bible and a newspaper in every house, a good school in every district, the principle support of civil liberty.

This sentence fragment, a paraphrase of a complete sentence spoken by Benjamin Franklin, lacks the verb *are* after the second comma. Always check a sentence to determine if it has a verb of action or being.

17.3. Fragments with Verbs That Are Not Predicate Verbs

The subject of a sentence always requires a predicate verb that activates it or provides information about it (see p. 59). Sometimes there are verbs in sentences that do not relate to the subject in this manner but to the various objects and completers involved.

Nicklaus, Palmer, and Trevino, under the awards tent, where they waited quietly for the round to finish.

Where is the verb that explains "who" was under the awards tent? Clearly, "waited" does not serve this function. A predicate verb must be added to complete the sentence.

Nicklaus, Palmer, and Trevino stood under the awards tent, where they waited quietly for the round to finish.

The way to correct such fragments is to locate the subject and then provide the matching predicate verb.

17.4. Fragments Caused by Incomplete Progressives (-ing Verb Forms)

A quick review of section 15.3 (see pp. 69–70) indicates that a complete progressive tense verb form will always have an *-ing* verb and a helping verb derived from *be*. An *-ing* verb form is a participle (*-ed* and *-en* are also participles), and a participle cannot serve as a predicate verb. When you mistake a participle for a predicate verb, the result is a sentence fragment.

Fragment Maria bringing the salad to the picnic.
Complete Sentence Maria is bringing the salad to the picnic.

The use of *-ing* verb forms in place of the predicate verb appears regularly in dialect, but in conventional writing it creates sentence fragments. The problem is easily corrected by combining the *-ing* word with some form of the verb *to be*.

17.5. Fragments Caused by Incomplete Past Participles (-ed, -en, and Other Irregular Verb Forms)

In order for it to function as a predicate verb, the past participle must be combined with some form of *to be* or *to have*. Without this combination, there will always be a sentence fragment.

The union members thrown the radicals out.

We seen them at Korvettes.

The equipment stolen from the college gym.

An avalanche triggered by the sonic boom.

All these are examples of fragments that lack key helping verbs like *have, had, was,* and *had been*. To correct this mistake, add the appropriate form of *to be* or *to have*.

17.6. Fragments Caused by Subordinating Connectives

One of the most common sentence fragments occurs when a subordinate clause (see pp. 98–100) is permitted to stand by itself. These clauses are signaled by subordinating connectives, which normally are subordinating conjunctions or relative pronouns. The trick is to remember that a subordinating clause, even if it has a subject and verb, involves an idea that is dependent on the major idea in a compound sentence. Here are some fragments that start with subordinating connectives:

Such as beating, mistreatment, or possibly being raped by the father.
Although child abuse may result from the way our parents treated us when we were young.
Because the sand is too hot to walk on without sandals.
For example, the decline in infant mortality.

What is clear about these sentence fragments is that none of them involves a complete thought. We expect something to come before or follow such fragments in order to make their meaning whole.

Hint: Connect a fragment involving subordinating connectors to the sentence that comes before it or after it, depending on which has a closer relationship to the fragment.

  A motorcycle can be operated safely. If you use proper skills. Correct

  $$\text{If you use proper skills.}$$
  $$\text{FRAGMENT}$$

training by experts is required.
  A motorcycle can be operated safely if you use proper skills. Correct training by experts is required.

Because the following words tempt us to create word groups that seem to be complete but actually are not, they should serve as signals that a complex sentence (see p. 61) is needed.

after	how	what
also	if	whatever
although	in order that	when
as	like	where
as if	once	wherever
as long as	provided	whether
as soon as	since	which
as though	so that	while
because	such as	who
before	that	whomever
especially	though	whose
for example	unless	whoever
for instance	until	

Most fragments are caused by carelessness or a lack of sentence sense. A careful proofreading (see p. 127) will catch many fragments caused by hasty writing. Additionally, the first two sections in this part of the *Handbook* should be read carefully by anyone who consistently writes sentence fragments.

Application 1   Rewrite the following fragments to produce complete sentences.

a. Drug abuse, the most critical reason for my neighborhood's decline.

_____

b. The Dallas Cowboys seen by the kids in the airport. _____

_____

c. Which occurred one April morning last year. _____

_____

d. As if the woman ever had a chance. _____

_____

e. I going to Canada for my vacation. _____

_____

f. Because the Rolls-Royce is a majestic car. _____

_____

g. Detroit, an older American city with monumental urban problems.

_____

_____

h. Walking down Broadway for five blocks until you reach Myrtle Avenue Station. _____

_____

i. For example, Las Vegas. _____

_____

j. Ray and Debbie having no problems in college this year. _____

_____

Application 2   As noted earlier in this section, fragments sometimes are used for special effect, especially in advertising, newspaper headlines, and signs. Locate three examples of such fragments and then rewrite them to form complete sentences. An example appears below.

a. Each pleasant tasting. Each pleasing to the eye. And each smooth and light to the palate.

Rewrite: Each is pleasant tasting, pleasing to the eye, and smooth and light to the palate.

b. _____

_____

_____

_____

c. _____

_____

_____

_____

d. _____

_____

_____

_____

CHAPTER 18

Fixing Comma Splices and Run-on Sentences

Comma splices and run-on sentences are the opposite of sentence fragments (see pp. 83–88). Whereas a fragment is *less* than a sentence, a comma splice or run-on is *more* than a sentence. A comma splice occurs when you have a comma between two independent clauses, but no coordinating conjunction *(and, or, but, for, nor),* or when you use a conjunctive adverb *(however, therefore, nevertheless, consequently)* with a comma to separate two independent clauses. A run-on sentence is two or more sentences that are pushed together without *any* punctuation when they should either be separate or linked by proper connecting words and punctuation. Comma splices occur more frequently in writing than run-on sentences. (A comma splice actually is a type of run-on sentence.) Both result from an improper knowledge of sentence structure, notably in the area of coordination.

An understanding of the following principles will help you to eliminate comma splices and run-ons:

1. *Connect the two clauses with an appropriate conjunction* (**and, or, but, for, nor, yet**).

Comma Splice   Politics confuses me, I don't know much about it.
Corrected   Politics confuses me, *for* I don't know much about it.

2. *Separate two clauses with a period instead of a comma.*

Comma Splice   In the 1890's they didn't have power boats like we have today, they used steamboats for transportation from one part of the river to another.
Corrected   In the 1890's they didn't have power boats like we have today. They used steamboats for transportation from one part of the river to another.

3. *Separate the two clauses with a semicolon (;) if they are closely related in meaning.*

Comma Splice Enroll in a special diploma program, in this way you might get a better job.

Corrected Enroll in a special diploma program; in this way you might get a better job.

> *Hint:* The semicolon carries the same weight or pause as the period, but can be used only to connect closely related ideas.

4. *Always use a period or semicolon before conjunctive adverbs that join two independent clauses.*

Comma Splice There is always the dream of success, however, it is increasingly difficult to achieve success today.

Corrected There is always the dream of success. However, it is increasingly difficult to achieve success today.

5. *Change one of the independent ideas to a dependent idea.*

Comma Splice The stranger approached swiftly, I was frightened.
Corrected Because the stranger approached swiftly, I was frightened.

> *Hint:* Comma splices are frequently caused by pronouns like *I* in this example or *they* in example 2 because they give the wrong impression that a single idea is continuing.

6. *Start the second independent clause with an -ing word.*

Comma Splice Monroe stopped at the circle, he passed quickly to McAdoo for the jumper.

Corrected Monroe stopped at the circle, passing quickly to McAdoo for the jumper.

7. *Where no punctuation separates two sentences, use any of the strategies listed above to correct the run-on.*

Run-on Why did so many New Yorkers support England during the Revolution this is a hard question to answer.

Corrected Why did so many New Yorkers support England during the Revolution? This is a hard question to answer.

Because comma splices and run-on sentences are frequently caused by the improper overloading of sentences with phrases and clauses, basic principles of coordination and subordination will be discussed in the next two sections.

Application Correct the following sentences, which have comma splices or run-ons in them. Try to use various strategies for correction.

a. Many states have passed the Equal Rights Amendment, however, there are several remaining states in which opposition to the amendment is strong. _____

_____

_____

b. "The church is the door through which we first walked into Western civilization religion is the form in which America first allowed our personalities to be expressed." _____

_____

_____

c. Scopes was prosecuted for teaching Darwin's theories, he was defended by Clarence Darrow. _____

_____

_____

d. Might makes right this is a sad fact of life. _____

_____

e. Distinguish yourself, speak good Spanish. _____

_____

CHAPTER 19

Principles of Coordination

You are already familiar with *coordination,* which involves the joining of two main ideas that are closely related and of equal importance in the same sentence. What you are actually doing is bringing two complete sentences together by linking them with *and,* another connecting word, or proper punctuation.

The sailboat capsized, and the passengers drowned.

| FIRST SENTENCE | SECOND SENTENCE |

Always use a comma between two independent sentences joined by coordinating conjunctions.

COORDINATING CONJUNCTION (other coordinating conjunctions include *but, for, or, nor, yet,* and *so*)

(*Note:* Sometimes a semicolon can replace the comma and coordinating conjunction.)

If we were to diagram the structure of such a coordinated sentence, it would look like this:

INDEPENDENT CLAUSE + COMMA + COORDINATING CONJUNCTION + INDEPENDENT CLAUSE

Notice how this pattern works for the following sentences:

He went to the supermarket, but he forgot to take his wallet.
Julio was watching "Borinquen Canta," for it was the best Spanish program on television.
Please be there at eight o'clock, or you will miss the start of the movie.
The contract seems valid, yet I doubt the company's motives.

The only departure from such a pattern can occur through the elimination of the comma when the independent clauses are very short. (The comma could have been eliminated from "The sailboat capsized, and the passengers drowned.") However, the clauses involved in the four examples above are sufficiently long to justify the inclusion of a comma.

There are certain paired conjunctions that we use from time to time in sentences involving two independent ideas. The most common of these correlative conjunctions are listed on page 55. They appear in compound sentences in the following way:

Either I will vote for someone who appreciates the problems of farmers, or I will
    vote for no one at all.

In using paired conjunctions, we must avoid the temptation to put more than one comma in the sentence: "Either, I will vote for someone who appreciates the problems of farmers, or, I will vote for no one at all." The two added commas in this sentence are unnecessary.

Once you have mastered coordination, you should not use it to excess. In other words, you should not overload sentences with excessive coordinating conjunctions.

Families, schools, and churches are important in creating a sense of community,
    but families are most important, *and* I come from a closely knit family, *so* I
    know the values that it creates.

Usually one coordinating conjunction in a sentence is an effective strategy. Here, the writer links four sentences with three coordinating conjunctions (in addition to the "and" which is used to separate items in a series). What is the effect? Overloading sentences with coordinating conjunctions creates a monotonous style. Moreover, it prevents writers from establishing the relative importance of ideas in such sentences.

In addition to coordinating clauses, it is also necessary to coordinate phrases in sentences. As you recall, a phrase is a group of words that lacks either a subject or a predicate. Phrases are classified as *participial phrases, prepositional phrases,* and *infinitive phrases.* The participial phrase often has an *-ing* form of the verb at its start and consequently is easily recognizable: "swimm*ing* in the lake"; "hav*ing* seen *Jaws* three times"; "falter*ing* at the start of the race." It often comes at the start of a sentence and requires a subject immediately after it:

Having seen *Jaws* three times, I still want to see it again.
PARTICIPIAL PHRASE   COMMA   SUBJECT   INDEPENDENT CLAUSE

> **Hint:** Avoid dangling participials (or *dangling modifiers*) that do not have proper subjects and consequently cause confusion and illogical relationships.
>   Having seen *Jaws* three times, the film is still exciting.
> Here, the film is doing the seeing! The reader might know what you mean, but there is a dangling modifier nevertheless.

Participial phrases can be formed from the past forms of verbs, in which case the *-ing* signal is replaced by the *-n, -en, -t, -d,* or *-ed* form of a given verb. (The example using *Jaws* actually involves present perfect forms.)

Forgotten too long by history, the American Indian has been rediscovered by

       PARTICIPIAL PHRASE

today's college students.

Coordinating participial phrases in sentences is a relatively easy procedure because the coordinating conjunctions typically involved are *and, but,* and *or.* (Paired conjunctions also can be employed.) Remember that the participial phrases which you join through coordination *must have the same subject.*

Breaking through the line and angling toward the sideline, O.J. Simpson was on

  PHRASE 1   CONJUNCTION   PHRASE 2   SUBJECT   VERB

his way to another touchdown.

> **Hint:** A comma is not needed after the first participial phrase.

   With prepositional phrases, which often appear within sentences rather than at the start of them, there is also a signal word—a proposition like *to, in, by, of*—that begins the phrase. (Consult the list of prepositions on pp. 53–54 for other examples.) In a prepositional phrase, the phrase itself always seeks an object, which is called *the object of the preposition.*

We went to the ball game.

     PREPOSITIONAL PHRASE

Fortunately, the same conjunctions that link participial phrases in sentences also link prepositional phrases, although at times the preposition will change.

We went to the ball game and to a diner afterward.

       PHRASE 1   CONJUNCT   PHRASE 2

Punctuation is not required when coordinating such prepositional phrases.

The third group, infinitive phrases, involves an infinitive linked to a completer. An infinitive can seldom serve as the subject of a sentence, although an infinitive phrase often can:

To be blond is not to have more fun.

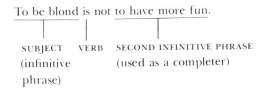

  SUBJECT   VERB   SECOND INFINITIVE PHRASE
  (infinitive   (used as a completer)
  phrase)

This example shows the two typical functions of infinitive phrases in sentences. When coordinating infinitive phrases in sentences, the conjunctions which you already are familiar with can be used. Moreover, as with prepositional phrases, coordinating conjunctions can be eliminated from infinitive phrases entirely.

To support President Nixon or not to support him is

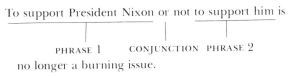

      PHRASE 1   CONJUNCTION PHRASE 2
no longer a burning issue.

To want to see beyond death is a common desire.

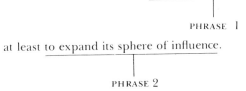

PHRASE 1 PHRASE 2
(no conjunction required)

The Soviet Union would like to dominate the world, or

                          PHRASE 1

at least to expand its sphere of influence.

              PHRASE 2

Coordinating phrases in sentences is a simple matter, as long as you do not make awkward shifts in the forms that you are using and maintain proper parallelism—both marks of smooth sentence structure (see pp. 119–121).

Application 1   Write coordinated sentences using the coordinating conjunctions given below. Vary the content of your independent clauses in each sentence.

a. and _____

_____

b. but _____

_____

c. for _____

_____

d. or _____

_____

e. either . . . or _____

_____

f. not only . . . but also _____

_____

Application 2   Develop complete sentences for the following coordinated phrases.

a. living in the suburbs but wanting to return to the city _____

_____

_____

b. attracted to Richard but repelled by his drinking problem _____

_____

_____

c. in triumph and in defeat _____

_____

d. from New York to Los Angeles _____

_____

e. neither with hope nor with conviction _____

_____

f. to value liberty yet to understand responsibility _____

_____

_____

g. having heard the Bee Gees and having seen Blood, Sweat and Tears in
concert _____

_____

CHAPTER 20

Principles of Subordination

Subordination involves the use of a main idea and a minor idea that is related to the main idea in a sentence. It is more useful than coordination, because two ideas are rarely of equal weight, which is what coordination requires. In subordination, only the main idea is a complete sentence that can stand by itself. The less important idea (the subordinate or dependent part) is not a complete sentence and cannot stand by itself.

Because of its well-preserved homes and gardens,

MINOR IDEA: NOT A COMPLETE SENTENCE

Charleston attracts many tourists who are interested in American history.

MAIN IDEA: COMPLETE SENTENCE

The "Because" which starts this sentence is one of many subordinators signaling the start of the minor or dependent idea. You have already seen how such subordinators can cause sentence fragments (p. 85) if the phrases and clauses that they introduce are not linked to main ideas that can stand independently as sentences.

Fragment   If you like grits for breakfast.
Corrected   If you like grits for breakfast,

MINOR IDEA (SUBORDINATE CLAUSE)

you should eat at the Southern Family Restaurant.

MAJOR IDEA: INDEPENDENT CLAUSE

Here, "If" signals the start of a subordinate clause that will depend upon an independent clause for the completion of meaning in the sentence.

Subordinators such as *if* and *because* are known as "danger words" because they create problems for writers who do not understand the principles of subordination. Subordinators, when used properly, add enormous variety and precision to your sentences.

Several subordinators have already been mentioned in this *Handbook*. A more extensive list of the most common subordinators appears below:

after	for instance	unless
also	how	until
always when	if	when
although	in order that	where
as	like	wherever
as if	near where	whether
as long as	now when	which
as soon as	once	while
as though	provided	what
because	provided that	whatever
before	since	who
close to where	so	whoever
especially	so that	whom
even	such as	which
even if	supposing that	whomever
even though	though	whosever
for example	toward where	

The dependent clause (minor idea) in a sentence, which is introduced by a subordinator, will be joined to the independent clause in one of two main ways:

DEPENDENT CLAUSE + COMMA + INDEPENDENT CLAUSE

or

INDEPENDENT CLAUSE + DEPENDENT CLAUSE

In practice, either pattern is effective, with the change from one method to the other rarely affecting the meaning of the sentence. The main point to remember is that when you start a sentence with a dependent clause, it should always be followed by a comma, whereas a comma is not needed when the dependent clause comes last.

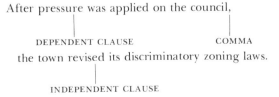

After pressure was applied on the council,
DEPENDENT CLAUSE   COMMA
the town revised its discriminatory zoning laws.
INDEPENDENT CLAUSE

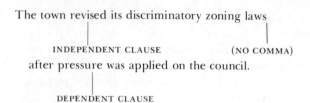

The town revised its discriminatory zoning laws

       INDEPENDENT CLAUSE   (NO COMMA)

after pressure was applied on the council.

       DEPENDENT CLAUSE

At times, a subordinate clause will not come at the beginning or the end of the sentence, but in the middle of it. A subordinate clause of this type will be introduced by *who* or *which:*

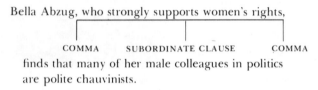

Bella Abzug, who strongly supports women's rights,

      COMMA   SUBORDINATE CLAUSE   COMMA

finds that many of her male colleagues in politics
are polite chauvinists.

Notice that this subordinate clause interrupts the complete sentence and is separated from it by two commas. Technically, the clause is *nonrestrictive,* which means that it adds information to the sentence that is not absolutely required. You point to the fact that the information in the clause could be left out by framing it with commas.

Hint: Do not use commas for clauses that give critically important information in the middle of a sentence.

    People who know about tennis have their

        SUBORDINATE CLAUSE

    rackets strung.

This type of subordinate clause is called *restrictive* because it limits the meaning of the word or words that come before it.

The ability to subordinate phrases and clauses effectively in sentences is a primary sign of competent writing. Moreover, subordination takes you away from the short, choppy sentences that are a sure indication of writers who are uncertain about their skills. Use subordination to reveal to the reader your mastery of sentence form.

Application 1 Write five sentences that begin with the subordinators that are listed. Be certain to provide commas for these sentences.

  a. Because _____

_____

b. Even though _____

_____

c. If _____

_____

d. Unless _____

_____

e. Before _____

_____

Application 2 Complete the following sentences by providing a subordinate idea.

a. Henry felt bored _____

_____

b. She behaves badly _____

_____

c. There is a large parking lot _____

_____

d. Service at La Fortuna is quick _____

_____

e. There will be problems at the atomic energy plant _____

_____

Application 3 Rewrite the following paragraph by using subordinators to link various sentences.

Moving out on my own was hard. I was only eighteen. I had a job. I earned seventy dollars a week. I looked for a place to live for several weeks. I finally got something decent and cheap. It was a small apartment in the Mission District. Utilities were low. Expenses would be manageable. A week passed. I had bought pots, pans, plates, silverware, and linen. My relatives were angry. They did not visit me. It was shaky in the beginning. I can laugh today and say it was well worth it.

_____

_____

_____

_____

Sub

CHAPTER 21

Success with Pronouns

As you know, a pronoun takes the place of or refers to another noun or pronoun. Although it is easy to recognize pronouns in sentences, they actually cause serious problems for writers and for speakers. Many pronoun problems involve agreement. Sometimes there is confusion about what or whom a pronoun refers to. Finally, there are considerations of case (see p. 49) that often create difficulties for writers. Guidelines for effective writing in all three categories—pronoun agreement, reference, and case—appear in the following sections, as well as a discussion of pronoun usage in speech and in writing.

21.1. Pronoun Agreement

Pronouns have to agree with the nouns they refer to. In addition, when they are used as the subject of a sentence, they must agree with the predicate verb. Singular pronouns must be used to refer to singular nouns, and plural pronouns to refer to plural nouns.

Sally likes her breakfast at precisely 7:30.

SINGULAR   SINGULAR
NOUN   PRONOUN

Several college libraries in the San Francisco area

PLURAL NOUN

have integrated their holdings.

PLURAL PRONOUN

These are relatively simple examples of pronoun agreement. However, there are more complicated instances of pronoun agreement; some of them are itemized below.

1. Use a plural pronoun to refer to two or more words joined by *and*.

Robert Frost and Langston Hughes wrote their

PLURAL SUBJECT   PLURAL PRONOUN

poetry in the language of the common man.

2. The following pronouns are singular. Therefore, when they are used as subjects, they must take a singular verb. This is another instance of what is called subject-verb agreement (see pp. 74–80).

anybody	neither
anyone	nobody
anything	no one
each	none
either	nothing
everybody	one
everyone	somebody
everything	someone

Everybody in class wants to see *One Flew Over the Cuckoo's Nest*.

SINGULAR SUBJECT   SINGULAR VERB

3. The pronouns *all, both, few, many, plenty,* and *several* are plural. When they are used as subjects, they take plural verbs.

Both of the cars were badly damaged.

PLURAL SUBJECT   PLURAL VERB

Hint: Until recent times, it was conventional to use the personal pronoun "he" to refer collectively to both men and women, or simply to exclude women from the meaning of a sentence. Today, the "he" should be changed to "he or she" wherever appropriate. An even better strategy is to change the singular subject to a plural one, with a corresponding change of the pronoun from singular to plural.

    Old style: If someone wants to find out about social security benefits, he can do so easily.

    New style: If someone wants to find out about social security benefits, he or she can do so easily.

    New style: If individuals want to find out about social security benefits, they can do so easily.

In a sentence like the first one above, and in many others, it is clearly
discriminatory to eliminate women from the meaning intended.

4. When two words are linked by *either . . . or, neither . . . nor,*
or *not only . . . but also,* the pronoun agrees with the noun that is
closest.

Neither Harriet nor Farideh places her faith in more than one God.

        SINGULAR NOUN   SINGULAR PRONOUN

Either the President or the generals will make their views prevail.

        PLURAL NOUN   PLURAL PRONOUN

5. Collective nouns (such as *class, family, group, team,* and *number*)
take a singular pronoun when the nouns are treated as a single unit.
They take a plural pronoun when the nouns refer to individual
members of the group.

The family will have its lunch at Nathan's.

(the entire   SINGULAR
family)   PRONOUN

The team went their separate ways after the game.

(individual   PLURAL
members)   PRONOUN

21.2. Pronoun Reference

Pronouns should always refer clearly to another noun or pronoun in a
sentence. The antecedent of the pronoun must be readily understood by
the reader. Otherwise, the meaning will be confusing, vague, or difficult
to understand. Here are several ways to avoid typical problems involving
pronoun reference.

1. *When using pronouns like* **his, her,** *and* **they,** *make certain that the noun
to which they refer is very clear.*

Unclear The President told the Secretary of State that the Soviet Union was
displeased with his recent remarks.
(Who made the remarks—the President or the Secretary?)

Revised   The President told the Secretary of State that remarks attributed to the Secretary had displeased the Soviet Union.

2. Do not begin a paragraph or essay with a pronoun that refers to the title of your paper or to a noun in the title.

Vague   This novel is a story of man against nature.
Revised   *The Old Man and the Sea* is a story of man against nature.

3. Do not use a pronoun without providing a written antecedent. You cannot assume that the reader will provide an antecedent for you.

Unstated Antecedent   Pacification failed in Vietnam because the United States Army could not prevent <u>them</u> from infiltrating the protected hamlets. (Who is "them"?)
Revised   Pacification failed in Vietnam because the United States Army could not prevent the Viet Cong from infiltrating the protected hamlets.

4. Do not use the pronouns it, that, this, and which in a manner that is broad and vague.

Broad and Vague   Television has relied heavily on violent police dramas for success. <u>It</u> has led to aggressive behavior in children.
Revised   Television, which has relied heavily on violent police dramas for success, has contributed to aggressive behavior in children.

21.3. Pronoun Case

As mentioned on page 49, certain pronouns have subjective, objective, and possessive cases. Mistakes with pronouns also occur when the wrong case is used. The following information should help eliminate confusion about pronoun case.

1. Use I, we, he, she, and they (not me, us, him, her, and them) as subjects and as pronouns that name the same person as the subject.

<u>We</u> adults try to balance work, school, and family obligations.
James and <u>I</u> will be going to Washington this weekend.
That was <u>she</u> in the audience.

2. Use me, us, him, her, and them as objects that help to complete the meaning of a sentence.

The fight excited <u>me</u>.   (not *I*)
The situation in Belfast disturbs Kathleen and <u>us</u>.   (not *we*)
The dean congratulated <u>us</u> freshmen for the Ecology Field Day.   (not *we*)

3. **Who** *is used as the subject of a verb.* **Whom,** *used traditionally as the object of a verb, is used consistently today only after a preposition.*

John Scowcroft, <u>who</u> has a Ph.D., is a top adviser at the Pentagon.
Carlos Cruz was the poet to <u>whom</u> I was referring.

Hint: Sometimes you can solve the *who/whom* dilemma by eliminating the pronouns entirely or by replacing them with *that.*
John Scowcroft, Ph.D. is a top adviser at the Pentagon.
Carlos Cruz was the poet that I was referring to.

21.4. Pronoun Usage in Speech and in Writing

In conversation, we frequently take liberties in using pronouns; some of these habits have been absorbed into written English, but others have not. Some examples of typical pronoun usage in speech and in writing are explored in this section.

1. *In writing, do not use pronouns that duplicate unnecessarily the subject of the sentence. This feature, which is standard in some dialects, is called prenominal apposition.*

Spoken That man in the grocery store, he looks suspicious.
Written That man in the grocery store looks suspicious.

2. *Do not confuse* **who, that,** *and* **which.** **Who** *refers to a person.* **That** *refers to a person, thing, or animal.* **Which** *refers to a thing or animal.*

In speech, there is a tendency to use *that* when referring to people, as in "Barbara and James are two individuals that confuse love and sex." Technically, this is correct in both speech and writing. However, in writing, it is best to avoid any overuse of the word *that* to refer to people.

3. *Do not confuse* **them** *(a personal pronoun) with* **those** *(a pronoun which points out persons or things).*

Spoken The police stopped them drivers.
Written The police stopped those drivers.

4. *Words such as* **ourself, themself, theirselves,** *and* **hisself** *appear in dialect but not in written English.*

Spoken He will take care of hisself.
Written He will take care of himself.

5. *In both speech and informal writing, the objective* me *replaces the subjective* I *in this sentence.*

It is me. (Instead of the technically correct "It is I.")

Application 1   Supply the missing pronouns for the following sentences.

a. Hernando left for the airport without taking _____ passport.

b. The New York Yankees, with _____ great power hitters of the past, have _____ type of batter in _____ current lineup.

c. If Americans take _____ elections seriously, then _____ should vote in _____ more often than _____ do.

d. Children with working parents quickly learn how to take care of _____ .

e. _____ did the student council elect as _____ president?

f. Richard Wright is best known for _____ novel, *Native Son*.

Application 2   Underline the correct pronoun in the sentences below.

a. (She, Her) and (he, him) are on the Dean's List.

b. The tutor helped Jim and (I, me) with our calculus.

c. The waves carried Alfredo and (she, her) toward the beach.

d. (They, Them) and (we, us) took our vacations together.

e. Josette and (she, her) visit the Virgin Islands every year.

f. Alicia and (I, me) were both born in November.

Application 3   Supply the correct pronouns for the following sentences.

a. Neither the advertising agency nor the protesters would alter _____ position.

b. Each decision that we make has _____ consequences.

c. The students were upset by _____ grades on the final examination.

d. Not only Kennedy but also Johnson committed _____ energies to the Civil Rights Movement.

e. The group was elated by _____ audience with John Chancellor of NBC.

f. People should protect _____ health by exercising regularly.

Application 4   Revise the following sentences in order to eliminate the vague and confusing pronoun references.

a. Unemployment is a problem of government, although it rarely solves it.

_____

_____

b. The Celtics and the Warriors have devoted fans, although they sometimes are shoddy.

_____

_____

c. Women with families and jobs should expect help from their husbands with them.

_____

_____

d. The new stress on vocational courses makes them better prepared for the highly competitive job market.

_____

_____

e. Linda noticed several students writing slogans on the walls and looked more closely at them.

_____

_____

CHAPTER 22

Using Adverbs and Adjectives Effectively

Adjectives help to describe or limit nouns and pronouns. On the other hand, adverbs help to describe or limit verbs, adjectives, or other adverbs; they fix the time, place, degree, cause, or manner of the action. Both adverbs and adjectives (see pp. 50–53) are valuable in writing because they make sentences more colorful and complete. However, in order to use adverbs and adjectives successfully, you must be able to compare them and to distinguish between them. The major areas of difficulty in using adverbs and adjectives are explained in this section.

22.1. Irregular Forms of the Comparative and Superlative

A small but significant number of adjectives and adverbs have special forms for the comparative and superlative degrees. These ten important words should be mastered:

Positive	Comparative	Superlative
	Adjectives	
bad	worse	worst
good	better	best
little	less	least
many	more	most
much	more	most
	Adverbs	
badly	worse	worst
far	farther	farthest
little	less	least
some	more	most
well	better	best

22.2. Avoiding Double Negatives

In speech—and notably in some dialects—more than one negative word occasionally or regulary appears in a sentence. This results in what we call a *double negative*, acceptable in spoken English, but not in written English. The words *not* and *never* are negative adverbs (words that deny, reject, or refuse). They should not be used with other negative words like *no, nobody, nowhere, none, nothing, neither, barely, hardly,* or *scarcely* in the same sentence.

Spoken   I didn't see nobody in the park.

TWO NEGATIVES

Written   I didn't see anybody in the park.

22.3. Confusion of Adverbs and Adjectives

There is a tendency, more evident perhaps in speech then in writing, to use adjectives instead of adverbs to modify verbs, adjectives, and other adverbs. This practice centers on such core words as those listed on page 110. The following points will help you avoid confusing adverbs with adjectives.

1. *Do not confuse the adverb* **well** *with the adjective* **good.** *The adverb* **well** *will answer the question "how" something is done.*

Wrong   The band played good.
Right   The band played well.

Hint: Well can also be used as an adjective, but only when it means "healthy," as in "He is feeling well."

---

2. *Always use the adverbs* **really** *or* **very,** *instead of the adverb* **real,** *to modify a verb, adjective, or adverb.*

Wrong   The car swerved real fast to avoid the bus.
Right   The car swerved very fast to avoid the bus.
Wrong   New York has made a real genuine effort to balance its budget.
Right   New York has made a really genuine effort to balance its budget.

3. *Do not confuse* **nearly** *and* **almost,** *which are adverbs, with* **near** *and* **most.**

Wrong Hiroshima was near destroyed by the atomic bomb.
Right Hiroshima was nearly destroyed by the atomic bomb.
Wrong City highways most always cut through poor areas.
Right City highways almost always cut through poor areas.

4. *Remember to use an adjective, not an adverb, after a linking verb* (**be, seem, appear, become, taste, look, feel**).

As you recall, what follows a linking verb describes the noun or pronoun. It does not answer the question "how" something is done.

Wrong I feel wonderfully.
Right I feel wonderful.

22.4. Faulty Comparisons

Sometimes the comparisons that we make between two items are incomplete or illogical. Always remember to complete a comparison or to make certain that the two things being compared are set up accurately.

Incomplete The Pittsburgh Steelers play better football.
Complete The Pittsburgh Steelers play better football than any other professional team.
Incomplete Thomas Paine wrote more important essays during the American Revolution than any person.
Complete Thomas Paine wrote more important essays during the American Revolution than any other person.

In the examples above, the addition of completing words makes the comparison accurate. However, there are also comparisons that are totally false because the wrong elements are being compared.

Faulty The prices at Macy's are more reasonable than Bloomingdale.
Corrected The prices at Macy's are more reasonable than those at Bloomingdale's.

In the faulty comparison, a department store is being compared with a price. Even when you can assume that the reader will know what you mean, it is necessary to provide the correct form of comparison in order to avoid a grammatical mistake.

Application 1 Supply the comparative and superlative degrees of the following adverbs and adjectives.

	COMPARATIVE	SUPERLATIVE
bad	_____	_____
ugly	_____	_____
honest	_____	_____
beautiful	_____	_____
certain	_____	_____
fair	_____	_____
exciting	_____	_____

Application 2   Rewrite the following paragraph, correcting all mistakes in the use of adverbs and adjectives.

Most all the people who attended the rock concert said that it had been real good. One or two individuals felt strong that they had had the awfulest time of their lives. Doubtless they objected to the sharpest heat and some fierce playing musicians, who didn't scarcely bother to improvise correct. They probably will be happiest as time goes by and will realize that the concert was better.

_____
_____
_____
_____
_____
_____
_____
_____
_____
_____
_____

CHAPTER 23

Choosing the Right Preposition

Selecting the correct preposition for a prepositional phrase or a standard expression can be troublesome sometimes. This is especially true for people who are not native speakers of English, but there are constructions which tend to give everyone trouble. The most difficult prepositions are those which we use most frequently: *at, by, for, from, in, of, on, to,* and *with*. Several expressions that are frequently used in writing appear below. Whenever you are uncertain about the correct preposition to employ in the literally hundreds of word groupings that require them, consult a dictionary for help.

accompany by	The indicted official was accompanied by an army of lawyers.
accompany with	The letter of acceptance was accompanied with the request that I reply promptly.
according to	According to the forecast, the weekend will be sunny.
accused by	Jim was accused by several classmates of violating the honor code.
accused of	He was accused of statutory rape.
admit to	Mary admits to the mistake in the design.
admit of	Table pool is a game which admits of few lapses in concentration.
agree in	Your shirt agrees in color with your pants.
agree on	The panel agreed on the need to increase farm price supports.
agree to	The union agreed to a contract calling for a cost of living adjustment.
agree with	I do not agree with the conservative notion that we should preserve the status quo.

agreeable to	The mayor was <u>agreeable to</u> the townspeople's request to stop all landfill operations.
angry at	Professor Brown was <u>angry at</u> the construction noise in the building.
angry with	Bernard always seems to be <u>angry with</u> his wife.
conform to	People tend to <u>conform to</u> the will of their political leaders.
conformity with	Young people no longer are in <u>conformity with</u> the ideas of their parents.
differ about	The audience <u>differed about</u> the quality of the performance.
differ from	Even though they look alike, a Cadillac <u>differs from</u> a Mercury.
differ with	I <u>differ with</u> you on the need to reduce welfare roles.
different from	Chinese communism is <u>different from</u> Soviet communism.
identical with	The quality of the beaches in South Carolina is <u>identical with</u> those in Florida.
independent of	The blacks in South Africa want to be <u>independent of</u> white rule.
in search of	Mankind is always <u>in search of</u> the ideal society.
need for	There is a <u>need for</u> low-cost housing in the suburbs.
need of	The family car is in <u>need of</u> a tune-up.
overcome by	He was <u>overcome by</u> the Arctic's freezing weather.
overcome with	Denise was <u>overcome with</u> delight when she learned of her acceptance to law school.
part from	George Wallace has threatened to <u>part from</u> the Democratic party more than once.
part with	The bankrupt millionaire had to <u>part with</u> his Rolls-Royce.
treat of	Franklin's *Autobiography* <u>treats of</u> his rise to fame from lowly origins.
vary from	The quality of a hamburger <u>varies from</u> one restaurant to to another.
vary with	Some experts think that a person's sexual drive <u>varies with</u> age.

For years, English teachers instructed students not to end a sentence with such common prepositions as *from, on, to,* and *at.* In practice, there is nothing wrong with the procedure of ending a sentence with a preposition. In fact, it often is the most natural sentence construction. We often ask, "Where are you from?" Similarly, we might write, "We had to take off our shoes at the Japanese restaurant before going in." Perhaps it is still more "elegant" not to end a sentence with a preposition. Today, however, much written prose resembles the rhythms of good speech, and our conversation is filled with sentences ending in prepositions.

On the other hand, there are areas in which we make frequent mistakes in the use of prepositions. The following list will help you to avoid some standard errors.

1. Don't use the preposition of in place of 've or have.

Wrong   The President should of increased revenue sharing.
Right   The President should have increased revenue sharing.

> *Hint:* One way to determine if any word is a verb is to put a pronoun before it and see if the word group makes sense. For instance, "I of" does not make sense. *Of* cannot function as a verb.

2. Don't confuse in and into. In means "already within."

He was working in the supermarket. (He was already there in the situation.)

Into means "from without to within."

He walked into the supermarket. (He was outside the area and then entered it.)

3. Don't confuse beside and besides. Beside means "next to."

When Karen stands beside Clyde, they resemble Mutt and Jeff.

Besides means "in addition to."

Besides the Yankees, the Red Sox and the Orioles make the East Coast the strongest area in professional baseball today.

4. Don't confuse between and among. Between is used to refer to two persons only.

In the 1960's, the rock empire was divided between the Beatles and the Rolling Stones.

Among is used to refer to three or more persons or things.

In the 1960's, the rock empire was divided among Bob Dylan, the Stones, and the Beatles.

5. Don't use off of for off.

Colloquial   They got off of the property.
Written   They got off the property.

6. Don't use at about for about.

Colloquial The job pays at about $3.50 hourly.
Written The job pays about $3.50 hourly.

7. Don't use at or to after where.

Colloquial Where will you go to after the game?
Written Where will you go after the game?

Application 1. Add prepositions to the following words and then use them in a sentence. If you have trouble selecting the right preposition, consult a dictionary.

a. absolved ——— ——————————————————

————————————————————————————————

b. argue ——— ——————————————————

————————————————————————————————

c. confide ——— ——————————————————

————————————————————————————————

d. disagree ——— ——————————————————

————————————————————————————————

e. live ——— ——————————————————

————————————————————————————————

Application 2 Rewrite the following sentences so that the preposition comes at the end.

a. To whom did you give the pen? ——————————

————————————————————————————————

b. Ethnic consciousness makes people aware of from where their parents came. ——————————————————

————————————————————————————————

c. Prior to coming to college, Detroit was the place in which I lived. ——

————————————————————————————————

d. *Redskin* is a word about which there is considerable controversy.___

_____

e. In which hotel in Puerto Rico are you staying? _____

_____

Application 3 Rewrite the following sentences, which have misused prepositions.

a. There was a conference among the players' association and league officials. _____

_____

b. He walked in the class late, trying to look cool. _____

_____

c. Bobby Kennedy would of made a good President. _____

_____

CHAPTER 24

Creating Smooth Sentences

The creation of smooth sentences depends on your mastery of material that has already appeared in this part of the *Handbook*. To do this also requires the ability to maintain a balance and consistency among certain elements in a sentence. Two prime obstacles to sentence smoothness are *faulty parallelism* and *unnecessary shifts*. These problems will be identified and discussed in the two sections that follow.

24.1. Faulty Parallelism

Faulty parallelism is the failure to repeat similiar words and word groups that are related to similar ideas. In other words, you should have identical grammatical forms to express parallel ideas. Look at the sentence below, which is an example of faulty parallelism.

Faulty Ernest Hemingway was both a writer and he liked to hunt.

There is no balance between the two parallel ideas—the fact that Hemingway was a writer and a hunter. If we were to put these ideas into parallel form, the sentence might look like this:

Smooth Ernest Hemingway was both <u>a writer</u> and <u>a hunter</u>.

Here, the underlined words parallel each other in form, creating a smooth, balanced effect. In addition, fewer words are involved in the smooth sentence than in the sentence with faulty parallelism. When a sentence is parallel, it is not only smooth but also economically written.

Here are some examples of correct parallelism. The parallel elements in each sentence are underlined.

She likes <u>apples, pears, and peaches</u>.
Give me liberty or <u>give me</u> death.
Although sportsmanship is important, it is better <u>to win</u> than <u>to lose</u>.
The horse <u>broke</u> from the starting gate, <u>headed</u> for the inner rail, and <u>raced</u> into the lead.

Parallelism can apply to words, phrases, and even sentences. It is especially necessary to maintain parallelism when using two or more verbs.

24.2. Unnecessary Shifts

In order to create smooth sentences, you also have to be consistent in the way in which you use certain grammatical constructions. For instance, you do not want to shift unnecessarily from one verb tense to another in a sentence. Similarly, you do not want to shift unnecessarily from the singular to the plural. There are many varieties of shifts that writers make without justification. The major shifts involve tense, number, and person.

With shifts in tense, the writer moves inconsistently from the present tense to the past tense, or from the past tense to the present tense.

Shift   I went to see *Funny Girl,* but I do not like it.
Consistent   I went to see *Funny Girl,* but I did not like it.

Shifts in tense can sometimes be complicated by the form of the sentence.

Shift   The miners went into the shaft, even though they know they will not be safe.
Consistent   The miners went into the shaft, even though they knew that they would not be safe.

Here, the writer did not realize that the tense of the main verb determines the tense of a verb in the subordinate clause. Verb tenses have to agree logically with each other in subordinated sentences.

The second type of shift, in number, results from an inconsistent use of singular and plural nouns and pronouns. Probably the most common shift in number involves a singular noun with a plural pronoun.

Shift   A politician is ambitious, but they don't have to be dishonest.
Consistent   A politician is ambitious, but he or she doesn't have to be dishonest.

Other shifts in number are possible—for example, from plural to singular—but the important thing to remember is to keep elements consistently singular or plural and not to mix them.

A third shift involves person. The chart for personal pronouns on · page 49 identifies first person pronouns *(I, me, we, us),* second person pronouns *(you),* and third person pronouns *(he, him, she, her, it, one, they, them).* A common shift in person involves the use of *we,* which is first person, with *one,* which is third person.

Shift   We should not hitchhike, because one might encounter violent individuals.
Consistent   We should not hitchhike, because we might encounter violent individuals.

Moreover, *you* (in the second person) causes problems when mixed with third person forms, notably *one*:

Shift   College students no longer seem to be fascinated by drugs, although you can still find dealers on most campuses.
Consistent   College students no longer seem to be fascinated by drugs, although one can still find dealers on most campuses.

Try to avoid needless shifts in person.

Application 1   Revise the following sentences so that elements are parallel.

a. I came. I saw. I am conquering. ⸺⸺⸺⸺

b. I like skiing, swimming, and to camp. ⸺⸺⸺⸺

c. W. E. B. Du Bois is a name that is famous to black Americans, to revolutionaries, and sociologists. ⸺⸺⸺⸺

d. Success in college requires intelligence, perseverance, and you must also have luck. ⸺⸺⸺⸺

e. Soap operas possess emotion to an extreme degree, suspense in large doses, and sex. ⸺⸺⸺⸺

f. I saw Tom Seaver, the Reds pitcher and who is also a sportscaster in the off season. ⸺⸺⸺⸺

Application 2   Revise the sentences below to eliminate all unnecessary shifts.

a. I am crazy over ice cream, but they make me fat. ⸺⸺⸺⸺

b. When you visit the museum, one should be prepared to make a
contribution in lieu of admissions. _____

_____

c. The recipe calls for half a cup of white wine, but I added a full
cup. _____

_____

d. Most basketball players are very tall, but a baseball player is not. __

_____

e. If we look at the test carefully, you will see that you did not answer
the question correctly. _____

_____

_____

f. A man should take pride in his job, but they shouldn't consider it
the most important thing in life. _____

_____

_____

g. *Wiz* was a black version of *The Wizard of Oz;* it is still playing on
Broadway. _____

_____

_____

CHAPTER 25

Mechanical Accuracy: Punctuation, Capitalization, and Abbreviation

Every sentence that you write requires mechanical accuracy—appropriate capitalization and punctuation. Basically there are two types of punctuation: punctuation *inside* the sentence and punctuation at the *end* of the sentence. Some punctuation (parentheses, brackets, and quotations) can come inside or at the end of a sentence. Here is a diagram of the main punctuation marks.

Inside		*Inside and outside*		*End*
,	comma	" "	quotation marks	. period
;	semicolon	[ ]	brackets	? question mark
:	colon	( )	parentheses	! exclamation
—	dash	. . .	ellipses	point
-	hyphen	'	apostrophe	

Each punctuation mark has a special function or role in making the meaning of a sentence clear. Punctuation also affects the rhythm of a sentence and the emphasis that we place on words and word groups.

25.1. End Punctuation

All sentences must end with a period, exclamation point, or question mark. Otherwise you will have a run-on sentence or a comma splice (see p. 89).

1. *The Period (.)*

The period is the most common form of end punctuation. Other uses of the period are given below.

after statements   India has a large population.
after abbreviations   Mr. Dunne, etc., B.A., Main St., St. Louis, A.M.
after mild commands   Give it to me.
after courtesy questions   Would you please forward the materials as soon as possible.

2. The Question Mark (?)

Use a question mark after a sentence that asks a direct question, but not after a sentence that asks an indirect question.

Direct question   Who won the 1939 World Series?
Indirect question   He asked who had won the 1939 World Series.

3. The Exclamation Point (!)

Use an exclamation point after a sentence that shows very strong emotions or issues a sharp command.

It was a fantastic weekend!
Don't interrupt!

Hint: Do not overuse the exclamation point in formal writing. For instance, you can get away with one "fantastic!" but not "great!" "monumental!" and "I was so excited!" all in one essay.

25.2. The Comma (,)

The comma is the most common form of punctuation inside a sentence. Think of it as a *short pause* in the movement of a sentence. We make similar pauses in speech; consequently, we should try to "hear" a pause when writing and use a comma accordingly. Commas are used in many situations, as indicated below.

1. To separate items in a series.

He was sick, angry, and depressed.
Officials claim that George Jackson escaped from his cell, ran toward the prison wall, and was shot before reaching it.

Hint: You must have at least three items in a series before you can use a comma to separate them.

2. *To separate two complete sentences joined by* **and, or, but, for, nor,** *or* **yet.**

There are many wealthy Cubans living in Miami, but there are many poor
   Cubans living there too.
The audience sat transfixed, and then it broke into enthusiastic applause.

3. *To separate adjectives of equal rank and importance.*

It was a cool, bright morning.

> *Hint:* One way to determine whether adjectives are of equal rank and
> importance is to reverse them. If the meaning is still the same, you
> need a comma.

4. *After introductory parts of sentences.*

   a. After single words of transition such as *moreover, however, similarly,
nevertheless, therefore,* and *indeed.*

Moreover, Mario Puzo is a fine writer.

   b. After short transitional expressions like "on the other hand," "in a
similar manner," "in other words," "for example," and "in fact."

For example, Stanford University has an excellent electrical engineering program.

   c. After *-ing* verbs that begin a sentence.

Trying to brake quickly, Bob Petty lost control of his racing car.

   d. After subordinated word groups.

Although many people are aware of the plight of the American Indian, there is
   still little action to improve tribal conditions.

   e. After mild expressions.

Yes, I remember it well.

5. *To separate words or word groups that interrupt the main idea of the
   sentence.*

Johnny Unitas, a former quarterback for the Baltimore Colts, is now a
   sportscaster.
Women's liberation, however, has yet to win the support of most American
   housewives.

The swimmer, stretching, won by a fingertip.

Advertising, which has a strong hold on the American mind, is like propaganda.

6. *In certain conventional places.*

a.	in numbers	10,000
b.	to separate day, month, and year	On Wednesday, April 29, 1975, the last American soldier left Vietnam.
c.	in correspondence	Dear Jane, Sincerely yours,
d.	in addresses	Dallas, Texas Hempstead, Nassau County, New York Paris, France
e.	to separate titles and degrees from a person's name	Henry Kissinger, Ph.D., once taught at Harvard.

25.3. The Semicolon (;)

The semicolon is very similar to the period in that it signals a full stop. It also signals a much longer pause than the comma. The semicolon is used only in very special instances, as indicated below.

1. *Between two independent clauses.*

Gambling in New York is big business; it is run both by government and by organized crime.

> *Hint:* You actually use a semicolon instead of *and, or, but, nor,* or *for.* Normally, you do not use both a semicolon and a coordinating conjunction.

2. *To prevent confusion in a sentence that has many commas.*

The following state politicians are considered liberals: James Arvin, a black lawyer from Stauton; Lucille Campell, a feminist from Brisbane; and Frank Ricardi, who seems to be to the left of his local constituency.

25.4. The Colon (:)

The colon usually is a mark of expectation. It directs the reader to material that comes after an opening statement and helps to explain the initial statement. Colons can be used in the following ways:

1. *To introduce a list, an illustration, or a summary.*

Cigarettes have been linked to the following diseases: cancer, high blood pressure, and heart attacks.

Lennie Bruce was certainly "sick": he believed that American justice would exonerate him.

In summary, we can state the following proposition: a balanced American foreign policy is needed in the Middle East.

2. *To introduce a long quotation.*

An article in *National Geographic* states: "Clouded by uncertainty, the actual route followed by the Israelites from bondage in Egypt to deliverance in the Promised Land has been the subject of endless scholarly debate—much of it intriguing, little of it provable."

3. *In specific places.*

a. after the opening in a formal letter	Dear Mr. Dolan:
b. between hours and minutes indicating time	7:15
c. between a title and a subtitle	*Jane: A Case Study*
d. between chapter and verse in the Bible.	Matthew 12:7
e. between act and scene in a play	Hamlet II: ii

Hint: Do not confuse the semicolon and the colon. A semicolon separates elements, while the colon introduces elements.

25.5. Parentheses ( )

Use parentheses to set off minor ideas or casual remarks. Such word groups can range from single words to entire sentences.

Chicago (the Windy City) has a balanced budget.

When parentheses occur at the end of a sentence, additional punctuation comes after the last parenthesis.

Persian art is delicate (a world in miniature).

When a complete sentence appears within parentheses, it is standard practice to put a period at the end of the sentence coming before the parenthetical statement and at the end of the sentence inside the parentheses.

> Langston Hughes was the foremost poet of the Harlem Renaissance. (This is not to say that the movement did not produce other fine poets.)

Parentheses should also be used to enclose numbers within sentences, references to other sources, and incidental information.

> According to Camus, we must (1) understand the absurd; (2) act upon our understanding of the absurd; and (3) embrace the posture of rebellion.

Hint: Note the positioning of semicolons in this sentence, and the fact that *and* introduces the last item in the numbered series.

> Naturalism (see Walcutt) is a complicated literary phenomenon.
> F. Scott Fitzgerald (1896–1940) gave us the term "the Jazz Age."

Sometimes you can put quite a bit of information inside parentheses—two or three sentences. Regardless of the amount of information, always make certain that there is a parenthesis at the start and one at the end. *Don't forget the second parenthesis.*

25.6. The Dash —

Dashes are used in sentences to emphasize an afterthought.

> Margaret Bourke White's famous collection of photographs is owned jointly by a site developer, a builder, a lawyer, and a woman who arranges estate sales—an unlikely group of photo collectors.

Notice that here the dash functions somewhat like a comma, but the pause is longer and consequently more emphatic. Two dashes can be used to set off material you want to emphasize within a sentence.

> Most tax provisions—on oil, Social Security, rebates, and housing—were approved by Congress.

Dashes should be used sparingly in writing. Moreover, they should not be confused with colons or used in place of periods as end punctuation.

25.7. The Hyphen -

A hyphen is used to separate or divide words. In writing and typing, two hyphens are used to make a dash. The single hyphen is used in the following instances.

1. *To separate certain combinations of words that function as one unit.*

mother-in-law	twentieth-century artist
twenty-two	un-American
three-fourths	good-looking man

2. *To divide words at the end of a line when there is not enough space to write or type the whole word.*

Recently an African student, long a resident in this country, confessed to a group
of his intimates that he did not trust the American Negro.

Words at the end of the sentence cannot be divided in any manner. Always check a dictionary to determine the proper way to divide a word you are uncertain about.

> *Hint:* Here are two basic rules for dividing words at the end of a line: divide only between syllables, and never divide a one-syllable word.

The use of the hyphen involves spelling rather than punctuation, but because it is a mechanical feature, it has been incorporated into this section of the *Handbook.*

25.8. Brackets [ ]

Brackets, which should not be confused with parentheses, are used to set off unquoted material that is placed within a quotation.

"Roughly 85 percent [of the inmates] are Negro, and most, like Donald Payne, are stuck inside because they are too poor to make bail."

Material placed inside brackets either comments on the quoted material or clarifies it.

P

25.9. Ellipses . . .

Ellipses show that material has been left out of a quotation:

"Women . . . are only struggling for air. . . ."

Notice that three dots are used for ellipses within a sentence and four dots are used for ellipses at the end of a sentence.

25.10. Quotation Marks " "

Quotation marks cause a number of problems in writing because they have precise relationships to other forms of punctuation. The basic rule governing quotation marks is that all direct quotations should be enclosed by them.

James Baldwin has written, "I had inclined to be contemptuous of my father for the conditions of his life, for the conditions of our lives."

However, you may have occasion to write quotations within quotations, in which case single quotation marks are put around the internal quotation and double quotation marks are put around the external quotation.

The candidate, attempting to exhort the crowd, exclaimed, "I endorse New Hampshire's motto, 'Live free or die.'"

Hint: Put periods and commas inside quotation marks and semicolons and colons outside them. Other marks of punctuation go inside or outside, depending on whether they are part of the quotation.

There are special instances in which quotation marks are used:

a. around the titles of poems, short stories, essays, newspaper and magazine articles, songs, and one-act plays

"Birches"
"The Use of Force"
"A Hanging"
"Desolation Row"

b. to indicate an ironic, sarcastic, or mocking tone

We know that Richard Nixon was a "patriotic" man.

c. to cite words that are used as examples in a sentence

Words like "groovy" should not be used in writing.

Do not confuse quotation marks with italics, which is treated in the next section. In addition, you should not use quotation marks to set off the title of a paragraph or essay that you are writing.

Finally, do not confuse direct quotation with indirect quotation.

Direct Quotation Roderick asked, "Have you listened to the latest *Chicago* album?"

Indirect Quotation Roderick asked if I had listened to the latest *Chicago* album.

Do not attempt to shift from direct to indirect quotation in the same sentence. Remember that direct quotation requires punctuation marks, but indirect quotation does not.

25.11. Italics

Italics is a form of underlining.

1. *Underline the titles of books, plays, films, newspapers, and magazines.*

The Daily News
Godfather II
Raisin

The Grapes of Wrath
Time

2. *Underline all foreign words and expressions that are not part of the English language.*

The Casa Samba will present O Grande Culiban et a Pequeña Miranda.

3. *Underline words and phrases for emphasis.*

I do not think that George McGinnis is better than Julius Erving.
In order to clean up the Great Lakes, we must fine the companies that are polluting them.

25.12. The Apostrophe '

Like the hyphen, the apostrophe relates more to spelling than to the structure of the written sentence. It is used in the following cases:

1. *To show possession.*

Italy's problems
Laura's happiness
women's fashions
Davis' garage

2. *In contractions (words that have one or more missing letters).*

it's = it is
I'm = I am
he'll = he will
don't = do not
haven't = have not

3. *To show possession with words of time and money.*

a dollar's worth of gas
this month's electricity bill

> *Hint:* When a noun ends in *-s* (whether it is singular or plural), the apostrophe comes after the -s. A second *-s* is not added after the apostrophe except to indicate the pronunciation of the word. Thus, in one example above, *Davis'* could also be *Davis's* because the pronounciation is Da-vis-es.

25.13. Capitalization

The key to the successful use of capitalization is to remember that it always points out something particular and special. For instance, the start of a new sentence is always special; to point this out, you must capitalize the first letter in the first word of every sentence. Here are some other rules that will help you with capitalization.

CAPITALIZATION RULES

1. People

the name of a specific person	Cesar Chavez, Malcolm X
titles that go with names	Mayor Daley, President Kennedy
titles that replace names	the Mayor, the President
the word *I*	I enjoy tennis.
the names of specific family members	Uncle Adolph, Dad, Cousin Bruce

Hint: Do not capitalize names of family members when a possessive pronoun like *my* or *his* comes before them.

---

2. Places

the name of a particular place	San Francisco, the South, Las Vegas, the East, Puerto Rico, Middle East

Hint: Do not capitalize north, south, east, or west when you are simply noting a general direction.

the names of special buildings and sites	the World Trade Center, the Acropolis, the Golden Gate Bridge
the names of specific rivers, mountains, and parks	Mississippi River, Rocky Mountains, Central Park
the names of particular streets	Beale Street, Market Street, Fifth Avenue
the names of planets, stars, and constellations	Mars, the Milky Way

Hint: Do not capitalize *earth, sun,* or *moon.*

3. Groups

the names of racial, ethnic, and national groups	Negro, Italian, Greek, American

Hint: Do not capitalize *white* and *black* when referring to people.

the names of political groups	Democratic Party, American Communist Party, the Weathermen
the names of religious groups	Methodists, Catholics, Black Muslims, Zen Buddhists

Hint: Capitalize the names of a particular god (God, Buddha, Allah), all words referring to God (His ways), and all religious writings (the Bible, the Koran).

the names of organizations, business groups, clubs, and sports teams	the Sierra Club, the Elks, the Los Angeles Dodgers
the names of movements	Black Liberation, Chicano Power, the March on Washington

Hint: Do not capitalize the names of social or economic groups (*middle class, aristocracy*).

4. Dates

the days of the week	Monday, Saturday
months	January, May, December

Hint: Do not capitalize the seasons: spring, summer, fall, winter.

holidays	the Fourth of July, Easter Sunday
the names of historical events	the Civil War, the Dark Ages, the Cuban Missile Crisis

5. Titles of publications

the titles of books	*Invisible Man, For Whom the Bell Tolls*
the titles of newspapers	*The Washington Post*
the titles of magazines	*Time, Newsweek, Playboy*
the titles of stories, poems, and plays	"The Road Not Taken," "I'm a Woman"

Hint: Do not capitalize *a, an,* and *the* or conjunctions in titles unless they are the first word in the title. Do not capitalize prepositions like *of, in,* and *for,* which have less than four letters.

7. First words

the first word in a sentence	See the snow.
the first word in a quotation	Thomas Paine said, "These are the times that try men's souls."
the first word in titles of novels, poems, and plays	*A Bell for Adano, Please Don't Eat the Daisies*
the first word after a colon (:), but only when the statement following the colon is long.	John Dewey once wrote: "A renewal of faith in common human nature, in its potentialities in general and in its power in particular to respond to reason and truth, is a surer bulwark against totalitarianism than is demonstration of material success of devout worship of special legal and political forms."
the first word and all nouns in the opening of a letter and the *first word only* in the closing of a letter	Dear Mr. Rockefeller:
	Yours truly, Very truly yours, Sincerely yours, Cordially yours

25.14. Abbreviations

In normal college writing, it is best to avoid abbreviations as much as possible. Here are some specific suggestions.

1. Do not end a sentence with *etc.* Introduce your list with "such as" or "including."
2. Do not write *&* for *and*.
3. Do not abbreviate the names of days and months (Mon., Sat., Feb., Nov.). Write the entire word.
4. Do not abbreviate weights and measures (lbs., oz., ft., yd.). Write the entire word.
5. Do not use abbreviated titles like *Dr.* by themselves.

wrong The Dr. diagnosed my problem quickly.

right The doctor diagnosed my problem quickly.

There are times when abbreviations must be used, however. Forms such as *Mr., Ms., Dr.,* and *Jr.* are used with proper names. Moreover, certain abbreviations like B.A. and Ph.D. (academic degrees) and B.C. and A.D. (with dates) are permissible. You can also use initials for an organization (CIA, UNESCO, NBA) after you have first given its name in full.

> *Hint:* When a sentence ends with an abbreviation, use only one period: Rome fell in 440 A.D.

Application 1 Compose sentences according to the instructions given. Be sure to use commas where they are needed.

a. Write two complete sentences joined by the word *and*.

_____

_____

b. Write a sentence that includes your complete address.

_____

_____

c. Describe a person by using three items in a series.

_____

_____

d. Describe today's weather by using two adjectives of equal rank and importance.

_____

_____

_____

e. Use a word group beginning with _Although_ to start a sentence.

_____

_____

_____

f. Write a sentence that has an "interrupter" in it.

_____

_____

_____

g. Write a sentence that starts with _However_.

_____

_____

_____

h. Write a sentence that begins with an _-ing_ word group.

_____

_____

i. Write two complete sentences joined by the word _but_.

_____

_____

_____

j. Write a sentence that gives your complete birth date.

_____

_____

Application 2 Punctuate the following sentences. All sentences require more than commas.

a. For his epitaph Jefferson wrote Here was buried Thomas Jefferson author of the Declaration of Independence of the Statute of Virginia for Religious Freedom and Father of the University of Virginia

b. Complete Social Security exists in Great Britain and the Scandinavian nations it is a matter of policy in communist states although their resources are not always equal to the task

c. In this era of possible shortages there is one consoling thought The New York Times seems to have an unending supply of self righteousness

d. The following are finalists in the competition Rodriguez Peru Yamamoto Japan Mansour Iran and Mauridas Greece

e. Illinois requires that the state bring an accused man to trial within 120 days or turn him loose a deadline that eases the worst of the court-house delays and the jail house jam ups that afflict other cities.

Application 3 Supply quotation marks (single and double as required) and other appropriate punctuation for all direct quotations in the sentences that follow. (An indirect quotation does not require quotation marks. *Example:* He said that he was tired.)

a. The President said This meeting is adjourned

b. The senator reported that he would not seek reelection

c. Tocqueville said that Americans suffer from what he termed a strange melancholy

d. Do not talk in class shouted Professor Winters

e. I expect observed Herman to have the car paid for by the end of the year

f. Robert Frost's poem Stopping by Woods on a Snowy Evening is familiar to many Americans

g. The English teacher commented Macbeth's speech which begins To-morrow and tomorrow and tomorrow is one of the most famous monologues in Shakespeare's plays

h. Will you complete your term paper on time asked Shirley

i. Muhammad Ali indicated that he had been out of shape for the Jimmy Young fight

j. It is an insult stated Mr. O'Brien I will not stand for such language

Application 4 Capitalize all necessary words in the following letter.

56-17 56th drive
maspeth, new york 13742
january 22, 1975

ms. clair williams
kent agency
16 east 42nd street
new york, new york 10017

dear ms. williams:

i read your announcement in *the new york times* of a vacancy at the chase manhattan bank with interest, and i would like to apply for it.

i have dealt with the public for two and one-half years as a hostess at the massachusetts institute of technology. i have also handled telephones for the educational council of new york. such public contact will make me, i believe, a valued member of the chase manhattan staff.

i am twenty years old, and am sure i can quickly adapt to bank requirements. as mentioned on the enclosed résumé, i am attending laguardia community college, long island city, where i have taken secretarial and accounting courses. you will find me neat, well spoken, conscientious, and alert.

if you are interested in my candidacy, please feel free to contact me on monday, tuesday, or thursday at 937-9200. on other weekdays, i can be reached at 894-3148.

sincerely,

patricia a. kayser

PART 3

PARAGRAPHS AND ESSAYS: Putting Sentences Together

Sentences rarely exist in isolation. The writer combines sentences—normally between three and twenty of them—into units that are called *paragraphs*. Sometimes, especially for papers in basic English courses, a single-paragraph composition will be all that you need to write. However, there are also classes in which you have to write essays, which are combinations of paragraphs designed and linked to produce longer compositions. Regardless of length or form, the paragraph is the most important unit of organization in writing. In order for the paragraph to function properly, it must have a single topic, a clear focus on that topic, and a sound method of organization. Therefore, you cannot simply leap into a paragraph—unless, of course, you are blessed with excellent writing abilities and a rare capacity to organize material mentally. This part of the *Handbook* presents strategies for planning and writing solid paragraphs and essays that will reflect accurately what you want to say about your subject.

CHAPTER 26

Getting Started: The Process of Writing

The process of writing is a very personal activity. Some people write rapidly and others slowly, some with ease and others with difficulty. Many people suffer from "writer's block"—the inability to get started, to discover an appropriate subject, to conceive of a paragraph running to a full page. On the other hand, there are individuals who are like verbal machine guns, filling pages at a remarkable rate; sometimes their aim is on target, and at other times it is considerably off the mark. In short, we have to acknowledge that writing involves emotional and mental processes and not just mechanical ones. Yet even as it is intensely personal, the process of writing has one universal element or goal—to take the writer from a starting point in a paragraph or series of paragraphs to an appropriate conclusion.

You can make the process of writing manageable by observing the following steps.

1. *Choose your topic or subject carefully.*

The topic should be of potential interest to you, even if it is an assigned topic. It should also be the right size for the assignment. For example, if an instructor asks you to write an extended paragraph on pollution, you must first decide what aspect of pollution you know something about and consequently feel comfortable with. You also must limit your subject; otherwise, you will be too general in your approach to the topic, remaining on its surface rather than penetrating into it. Here, the generality triangle mentioned earlier in connection with vocabulary (see p. 17) also helps you to narrow a subject. You can't say much about pollution in the United States in a single paragraph. Moreover, it would even be difficult to deal effectively with all varieties of pollution in a major city like New York or Los Angeles. *One aspect* of pollution on your street or in your neighborhood, or perhaps in your town, is the right size for such an assignment. Before you start to write, have an idea of how you are going to limit and focus your topic.

2. *List ten or more ideas, details, questions, and strategies about your topic.*

Don't worry about the random order of the list. Try to let your mind roam over the topic for a few minutes. Every time you have the barest thread of an idea, jot it down. If it is hard to think of anything, *force* yourself to think of something and write it out, even if it seems absurd or does not relate directly to the topic. Remember the value of personal experience in helping to make a topic concrete. Also try to recall information from newspapers, newsletters, magazines, radio, television, and conversations. Here is a random list of ideas on the subject of pollution:

a. limit to my community?
b. water pollution—recycling—garbage—dumping?
c. most important issue—garbage dumping in sandpits.
d. dumping ground for whole county, but only my community suffers
e. former beauty of area
f. provide history of sandpits?
g. local groups opposed to dumping garbage in the pits: "Dump the Dump" stickers appearing.
h. what are politicians doing about it?
i. smell
j. appearance of rats, mice, gulls, other scavengers
k. seepage into water
l. why doesn't incinerator handle all garbage?
m. city and state regulations
n. future plans for sandpits
o. need for overall plan for their use

Ultimately, some of these items might be discarded, and others combined; some material might even be added. You certainly would want to rearrange the list somewhat. But at least a substantial step has been taken toward assembling information on the topic.

3. *Decide what main idea will hold most of your information together.*

Write this main idea in a complete sentence at the start of your paper. The one sentence that expresses the main idea in a paragraph is called a *topic sentence* (which will be discussed in greater detail in the next section). For a paragraph on pollution, a main idea could be this:

> Port Washington currently suffers from a growing pollution problem— the increasing amount of garbage from throughout the country that is being used to fill in the sandpits along the shore.

Several items from the basic list have been brought together to create this topic sentence, which should serve as the first sentence in your paragraph.

4. *Eliminate any points in your list that do not relate to the main idea.*

Also eliminate any material that might be too obvious, boring, or unimportant. Reconsider items that you do not know very much about.

5. *Number each remaining item in the order that you think it should appear in the paragraph.*

This revised order will be the plan for the written paragraph. It should reflect a careful *progression* based on a logical movement in time, space, relative importance of ideas, or the general and specific nature of the materials. For instance, if you were asked to write a brief autobiography, you would not want to describe your birth, then your present life, then a bad accident when you were in high school, then your admission to college, and then your First Communion. There is no order here, merely a random jumping from point to point in time. By numbering each item in your list, you will avoid faulty or loose progression.

6. *Write the paragraph.*

a. Put the topic sentence first.
b. Write complete sentences in the middle part (or body) of the paragraph based on your numbered list. Make certain that you incorporate enough material to make a solid paragraph.
c. Devise a good sentence to end the paragraph with. This is sometimes called a "clincher" sentence. It might be formed from the final item on your list, or it might be something that you develop at the last minute. (See pp. 154–155 for a discussion of the clincher sentence.)

The steps in writing that have been given can help many people. At the same time, the process of writing admits many personal strategies. If you write best while watching two television programs simultaneously on two sets, then follow this procedure if it produces good results.

Guidelines for Good Paragraphs

1. Always start a paragraph by indenting—by moving in the first line one inch (or five spaces on the typewriter).
2. Make certain that there are no writing mistakes in the sentences that make up the paragraph. Try to avoid common mistakes involving verbs, sentence fragments, run-on sentences, punctuation, capitalization, and missing words.
3. Try to have one sentence that expresses the main idea (the topic sentence) of the paragraph.

4. Stick to the main idea throughout the paragraph. Do not introduce other topics.

5. Make certain that you have enough material to support and develop fully the main idea. Avoid short, choppy paragraphs of only one or two sentences. Arrange your details in such a way that there are always connections between sentences and a building up of facts and information from sentence to sentence.

Application 1 Develop a "generality triangle" for any subject that is of interest to you and one that you know quite a bit about.

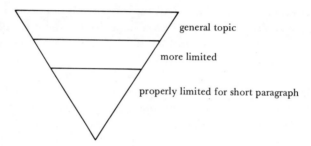

general topic

more limited

properly limited for short paragraph

Application 2 Take the limited topic at the tip of your triangle and jot down at least ten ideas about it.

a. _____

b. _____

c. _____

d. _____

e. _____

f. _____

g. _____

h. _____

i. _____

j. _____

Application 3 Establish a main idea for your topic and write it out as a full sentence.

_____

_____

Application 4   Revise your list by eliminating any item that you don't want to use and by numbering the remaining items in the order that you think they should appear in the paragraph.

Application 5   Write the paragraph. Have it consist of the topic sentence, at least three sentences in the body, and a clincher sentence.

_____

_____

_____

_____

_____

_____

_____

_____

_____

_____

CHAPTER 27

The Topic Sentence

You already know something about the topic sentence, which expresses the main idea in a paragraph. Accomplished writers occasionally permit the main idea to grow out of the entire paragraph without stating it in a single sentence. However, for beginning writers, there should always be a topic sentence in a paragraph. Although in practice you can place a topic sentence anywhere, it is best—so that you won't forget it or fail to focus on the topic quickly—to use it as the first sentence in the paragraph.

The major functions of a topic sentence are given below.

Five Tips for Topic Sentences

1. The topic sentence must *introduce* the subject to the reader.
2. The topic sentence must *limit* the subject.
3. The topic sentence must *express the writer's opinion* about the subject. This attitude or opinion can be very personal (subjective), detached (objective), humorous, serious, or ironic.
4. The topic sentence must *arouse* the reader's interest.
5. There must be *only one* topic sentence for each paragraph.

In the following short paragraph, taken from "The Pill and Modern Woman" by Robert Osterman and Mark Arnold, examine the function of the topic sentence, which has been underlined.

> <u>In recent years two proposals, working hand in hand, appear to offer the best means of solving the bulging problems of the poor and over-populated nations.</u> The first is to set up comprehensive birth-control campaigns to cut back their rising populations. At the same time they must develop natural resources, intensify economic growth, and promote the social welfare of their underprivileged masses.

This topic sentence is especially effective because it "hooks" us; we want to know about the two proposals (which serve as a limiting device), and consequently we are drawn by curiosity into the rest of the paragraph.

A successful topic sentence must fulfill several functions and in addition be properly written. The topic sentence must be a *complete* sentence. Nothing disturbs a teacher more than to see a sentence fragment serving as a topic sentence:

Fragment   Why entertainers in America earn too much money.

Sentence   Entertainers in America, whether they are movie idols, sports heroes, or rock stars, are among the most overpaid and overpriced individuals in society.

A topic sentence is not a shorthand note on the subject. It is a fully rounded statement of the subject and should be clear, direct, precise, and complete.

Application 1   Write topic sentences for the following subjects.

Example: *Student power*   Student power, once a rallying cry for college activists, has lost much of its appeal in the 1970's for three basic reasons.

Hint: One simple but effective way to limit your topic is to use expressions like "for three main reasons," "can be divided into two basic categories," and "are alike in several specific ways."

---

a. computers _____

_____

b. witchcraft _____

_____

c. drugs _____

_____

d. violence _____

_____

e. women's liberation _____

_____

f. racism _____

_____

g. music _____

_____

h. the Super Bowl _____

_____

i. unemployment _____

_____

j. day care _____

_____

Application 2   Revise the following topic sentences, which are incomplete or too general, weak, or vague. Be prepared to explain what you have done to make the topic sentences more effective.

a. How I spent my summer. _____

_____

b. In my opinion, abortion is a crime and a sin._____

_____

c. "All in the Family" is an excellent television program._____

_____

_____

d. Why do food prices keep going up?_____

_____

_____

e. The criminal is like a parasite. _____

_____

Application 3   Bring to class three illustrated advertisements. Write good topic sentences for these ads that introduce the product, express an opinion about it, and arouse the reader's interest.

a. advertisement 1: _____

_____

b. advertisement 2: _____

_____

c. advertisement 3: _____

_____

CHAPTER 28

Organizing the Paragraph: Development, Unity, Coherence

Once you have written a good topic sentence, you must then *develop* the paragraph. A properly developed paragraph provides enough support for the topic sentence. It presents the facts, details, and ideas in your basic list to reinforce the main idea expressed by the topic sentence. For a well-developed paragraph, *there must be enough material,* and this material must be organized in an effective manner.

If we use the topic sentence on student power, appearing in Application 1 on page 147, we can see how the process of paragraph development works.

Topic sentence	Student power, once a rallying cry for college activists, has lost much of its appeal in the 1970's for three basic reasons. In the first place,
Major support 1	the end of the Viet Nam war removed the main impulse that brought college activists together and made "student power" an issue of national debate. Moreover, the severe racial disturbances of the 1960's,
Major support 2	which began in the cities but quickly involved students on numerous college campuses, have not been repeated in this decade. It is
Minor support for 2	true that recent events such as those in Boston have revealed the persistence of racism in this country. However, no broadly based college student coalition has emerged to fight for integration in the
Major support 3	Boston schools. Finally, the increasingly bleak economic picture in the 1970's has forced students to attend to bread-and-butter issues. The
Clincher sentence	college activists of the 1960's have seemingly turned in their protest signs for diplomas in engineering and business—meal tickets that will help them to survive in an uncertain American future.

In this paragraph, the student has been careful to develop the topic sentence fully through the use of major and minor details. She fulfills the main idea expressed in the topic sentence.

> *Hint:* Avoid underdeveloped paragraphs by providing complete information about your topic. Make certain that your typical paragraph has a minimum of five sentences.

The paragraph on student power reveals two additional features of good paragraph organization—*unity* and *coherence*. To achieve unity, the writer must concentrate on only one subject in a paragraph and use material that is relevant to the topic sentence. One common characteristic of much college writing is a tendency on the student's part to wander from the subject or topic, as in this paragraph:

> My writing teacher is a very nasty person. He assigns too much homework and he is a hard grader. He lives in Elmhurst with his wife and pet cat. We never talk in class because he forbids it. College is a drag.

The underlined sentence violates paragraph unity because it gives un-necessary information about the topic. Moreover, the clincher sentence also weakens the unity of the paragraph by moving too abruptly (and too colloquially) to a general statement about the student's attitude toward college. In contrast, the paragraph on student power contains only in-formation that bears directly on the topic.

Coherence is also a feature of the paragraph on student power. To achieve coherence, all sentences must relate to each other in a logical way. Thus the paragraph progresses from point to point, and items have clear connections between and among them. There are three basic strategies for achieving such coherence, and they are reflected in the paragraph under discussion.

1. *Repeat key words, phrases, and expressions.*

By repeating key words and groups of words, the writer can keep the subject and crucial ideas before the reader. In the paragraph on student power, key words like "student power," "college activists," "students," and the "1960's" and "1970's" force the reader to maintain an awareness of their importance and significance.

2. *Use pronouns to maintain coherence.*

Pronouns (see pp. 48–50, and 103–107) can keep people, places, and ideas introduced in a paragraph fresh in the reader's mind at a later point. However, it is worthwhile to recall an earlier suggestion: always make certain that your pronoun reference in sentences and paragraphs is clear.

3. *Use transitional words and expressions.*

This is an excellent way to link sentences and ideas. Transitions are bridges from one part of a sentence to another, or from sentence to sentence. They exist in several categories, as is indicated in the following chart. Consult it whenever you need a transitional word or phrase.

TRANSITIONAL WORD CHART

Words to use

To show addition:

again, also, and, and then, another, besides, equally, equally important, finally, first, further, furthermore, in addition, in fact, in the second place, likewise, moreover, next, on top of that, secondly, third, too

To give examples:

as an illustration, as proof, especially, for example, for instance, for one thing, frequently, in general, in other words, in particular, in this way, namely, occasionally, specifically, that is, to illustrate, thus, usually

To show purpose or reason:

for this purpose, for this reason, to this end, with this object.

To show comparison (likenesses):

at the same time, in the same way, similarly, in like manner, just as, just like, likewise

To show contrast (differences):

and yet, although true, at the same time, but, conversely, despite, even though, for all that, however, in contrast, in spite of, nevertheless, notwithstanding, on the contrary, on the other hand, rather, still, whereas, while this may be true, yet

To grant a point:

after all, although, although this may be true, at the same time, certainly, doubtless, even though, granted that, I admit, I concede, in spite of, naturally, no doubt, surely, though, while it may be ture

To summarize:

accordingly, as a result, as has been stated, as I have shown, consequently, finally, in brief, in conclusion, on the whole, in short, therefore, thus, to conclude, to summarize

To show reason:

because, since, for

To show time:

after, afterward, at length, at last, before, earlier, finally, first, gradually, immediately, in the meantime, later, meanwhile, next, now, previously, second, soon,

Words to use

subsequently, suddenly, then, today, tomorrow, when, yesterday

To show position:

alongside, around, above, across, adjacent to, below, beyond, far, far away, in the background, in the foreground, inside, near, nearby, nearer, opposite, outside, surrounding, to the left or right, under

To show cause and effect:

accordingly, as a result, because, consequently, due to, hence, since, so therefore, thus

To emphasize:

again, indeed, in fact, surely, to repeat, truly

To show result:

all in all, after all, and so, as a consequence, as a result, at last, consequently, finally, hence, in conclusion, so, therefore, then, thus

---

Application 1 Number each sentence in the order that it should appear in the paragraph. Put an X next to any sentence that should be eliminated.

_____ a. In the spring, the boardwalk begins to fill with people.

_____ b. On Sunday I go to church, and during the week I work and attend college.

_____ c. The view from my kitchen window reveals to me how things change from season to season.

_____ d. At this time, my mind gets caught up in the sand and waves and I imagine that I am traveling to the Indies.

_____ e. When this dream is over, I know that fall is here, with the leaves turning brown in the trees along the boardwalk.

_____ f. Columbus thought that he had discovered the Indies.

_____ g. Next, in summer, these people are seen on the sand and in the waves.

_____ h. Finally, in winter the beach is deserted and the water looks dark and forbidding.

_____ i. For years, this has been the view from my window—my own personal calendar of the seasons.

Application 2　Take one of the topic sentences that you wrote on page 147 and organize a paragraph of six to eight sentences around it. Be prepared to explain why you think that the paragraph is properly developed, unified, and coherent.

_____

_____

_____

_____

_____

_____

_____

_____

_____

_____

CHAPTER 29

Ending the Paragraph

One of the most common mistakes in writing paragraphs (and essays as well) is the absence of an appropriate ending. Paragraphs frequently "dangle," leaving the reader confused or in suspense. You always have to end a paragraph on a note of finality, to finish it in an effective way. The reader must be left with the impression that the paragraph is complete in itself, and this feeling will not develop unless there is a "clincher" sentence. Here are some useful strategies for ending a paragraph.

1. *Employ signals that this sentence will bring the paragraph to an end.*

Words like *in conclusion, to summarize,* and *finally* are useful in beginning a clincher sentence.

2. *Simply rephrase the topic sentence.*

This is a somewhat mechanical procedure, but it can be effective in longer paragraphs, where the reader might forget the substance of the main idea. For instance, the sentence that you should have numbered last in the exercise on page 152 ("For years, this has been the view from my window—my own personal calendar of the seasons") is actually a reworking of the topic sentence ("The view from my kitchen window reveals to me how things change from season to season"). Do not rephrase the topic sentence in a very short paragraph.

3. *Add a final detail that rounds out the topic or prepares the reader for the next paragraph.*

In the following paragraph from *Malcolm X Speaks,* the clincher sentence involves a last detail, and also points toward possibilities and solutions that exist beyond the paragraph.

Not only does America have a very serious problem. America's problem is us. We're her problem. The only reason she has a problem is she doesn't want us here. And every time you look at yourself, be you black, brown, red or yellow, a so-called Negro, you represent a person who poses such a serious problem for America because you're not wanted. Once you face this as a fact, then you can start plotting a course that will make you appear intelligent, instead of unintelligent.

4. End with a question that deliberatly leaves the subject open or forces the reader to think about the topic.

Geronimo was the most famous of the Apache chiefs. He grew up at peace with the white race, until Mexican soldiers killed his wife and children. Geronimo, in retaliation, embarked on several campaigns against Mexican towns that resulted in many civilian deaths. Yet can we blame a man's desire for revenge when his entire family has been destroyed?

5. Use a quotation that rounds out and supports the topic.

If feminism is defined as the belief that women are human beings and entitled to the same opportunities for self-expression as men, then America has harbored a feminist bias from the beginning. In both the eighteenth and nineteenth centuries foreign travelers remarked on the freedom of women in America. "A paradise for women," one eighteenth century German called America, and toward the close of the nineteenth century Lord Bryce wrote that in the United States "it is easier for women to find a career, to obtain work of an intellectual as of a commercial kind, than in any other part of Europe."

CARL N. DEGLER
"The Changing Place of Women in America"

There are also many other ways to end a paragraph: using irony (saying or asking one thing, but actually meaning the reverse, as in the example on p. 162); reworking a well-known expression ("This just goes to prove that although you can't teach an old dog new tricks, you can teach an old human being new tricks"); and employing humor or shocking climaxes. Try to perfect as many concluding strategies as possible so that you can select the best ending for any paragraph.

Application 1   Write three different concluding sentences for the paragraph below.

Affirmative action programs have not been successful in the last decade. They have been costly, poorly administered, and ineffective. In fact, they have done little to advance the position of women and minorities. Institutions have established vague timetables for hiring more minorities and women, such as one college's decision to hire one-half of an Oriental in sociology within the next decade.

a. _____

  _____

b. _____

_____

c. _____

_____

Application 2   Bring to class three examples of good clincher sentences that you have located in your reading. Analyze the nature of each clincher sentence and the reasons for its effectiveness.

CHAPTER 30

Organizing Paragraphs Through Patterns

When we write paragraphs, we usually rely on certain organizational plans or patterns. The most common of these patterns are description, narration, example, comparison and contrast, classification, definition, and simple analysis. Sometimes we use just one of these patterns to develop a paragraph. At other times, we work with combinations of them. By mastering these patterns, you will be able to organize material on any subject more easily.

30.1. Description

Description involves the creation of a picture by using words. It focuses on objects, persons, scenes, and things that are happening. It appeals to the reader's sense of smell, touch, sight, sound, and taste. Quite frequently, description is used with other patterns of writing—especially narration.

Here is a very short paragraph of almost pure description:

The canyon is a ladder to the plain. The valley is pale in the end of July, when the corn and melons come of age and slowly the fields are made ready for the yield, and a faint, false air of autumn—an illusion still in the land—rises somewhere away in the high north country, a vague suspicion of red and yellow on the farthest summits. And the town lies out like a scattering of bones in the heart of the land, low in the valley, where the earth is a kiln and the soil is carried here and there in the wind and all harvests are a poor survival of the seed. It is a remote place, and divided from the rest of the world by a great forked range of mountains on the north and west; by wasteland on the south and east, a region of dunes and thorns and burning columns of air; and more than these by time and silence.

— N. SCOTT MOMADAY
House Made of Dawn

What is the difference between this short paragraph and a sentence like "The valley is empty and the town seems very lonely"? Basically, the paragraph permits the reader *to see* more clearly than the mere sentence the details of the scene. Good description will always be like the clearest of photographs.

The following are *rules for good description.*

1. Choose words carefully.

Try to select words that are sharp and clear—that appeal to the reader's senses. Don't be too general or abstract (see pp. 14–18) in selecting your words.

2. Choose details carefully.

You simply cannot describe everything in a scene. Try to pick only those details that are most useful in building your word picture.

3. Always create a main impression.

The main impression functions very much like the topic sentence. Try to organize your details so that there is a clear effect, rather than a blurred one. A main impression might concentrate on a very small point, or it might involve (as it does in the Momaday paragraph) a whole set of descriptive details that convey a special emotional mood or feeling to the reader.

4. Always move clearly from point to point in your description.

Don't jump around in a senseless way. Move carefully over details, almost like a camera moving over a scene. Try to present your details as the eye would pick them up. For instance, if you are describing a scene, you could move in an orderly manner from left to right, or from close up to far away. There are many ways to present description, but try to select that strategy that seems the most orderly.

Application Write a five- to ten-sentence descriptive paragraph based on the following photograph:

_____

_____

_____

_____

Wide World Photos

_____

_____

_____

_____

30.2. Narration

Narration is the telling of a story. It answers the question: "What happened?" Narration can be used in a wide range of writing situations. It can be used to tell real or fictional stories; to retell historic events; to relate a personal experience; to support an analysis of something. Narration almost always involves a fair amount of description. And it always involves the reader in _action_.

In order to make narration effective, you should observe the following guidelines.

1. _Always have a beginning, middle, and end to your narrative._

A story traces action over a period of time. Within that period of time, the action will start; it will develop; and it will complete itself. Don't break off the action in the middle of things.

2. _For single paragraphs, make the action concentrated._

Focus on a single incident that takes place in a short period of time. Don't try to narrate a broad event. Topics like "My Summer Vacation" or "My Life" are too vast to be treated effectively in one paragraph.

3. _Try to make the reader relive the story._

Learn to _dramatize_ the action by employing verbs of action. Introduce _conflict_ into the narrative. Use dialogue (speech in quotations) to support the action. With narrative, you can never risk being dull.

4. _As with description, good narration will select details of the action very carefully._

Don't introduce anything that is not worthwhile. Each detail or stage in the action should contribute to the meaning and the final effect of the paragraph.

Here is a sample paragraph involving narration.

HYPOCRISY

As the passenger entered the train, he noticed the scraps of paper and trash littering the floor. He brushed aside a blackened banana peel and sat down. "Damned pigs," he said; people next to him nodded. He opened his newspaper; while reading, he mumbled about the swine who were turning the city into a garbage dump. When he approached his station, he got up violently and stalked out. The wind from the rush of the train blew his paper onto the floor, where its pages began to spread like a dirty rain.

Application 1   Answer these questions about the paragraph you have just read.

a. How much time passes in this story? _____

_____

b. What is the writer's main purpose in telling the story? _____

_____

c. In what ways does he criticize the actions of people? _____

_____

d. Is there conflict in the story? If so, what kind? _____

_____

e. How does description help the story? _____

_____

Application 2   Look again at the photograph on page 159. Write a one-paragraph story based on the situation in that photograph. Try to include some of the material developed earlier in your descriptive paragraph.

_____

_____

_____

_____

_____

_____

Application 3 Write a paragraph that tells of the most frightening episode in your life. Remember: don't explain it; try to re-create it.

30.3. Example

Good examples help to make ideas clear and concrete; otherwise, these ideas would be vague and unsupported generalizations. A *generalization,* which is a broad statement lacking any support, always requires examples to make it effective. Although a paragraph can be organized exclusively around examples, it can also reveal examples mixed with other plans of development, especially comparison and contrast, definition, classification, argumentation, and analysis.

Examples can be developed in two basic ways. First, an *extended example* (one long example) can support an idea.

Moving leads to the termination of relationships in almost all categories. The young submarine engineer who is transferred from his job in the Navy Yard at Mare Island, California, to the installation at Newport News, Virginia, takes only his most immediate family with him. He leaves behind parents and in-laws, neighbors, service and tradespeople, as well as his associates on the job, and others. He cuts short his ties. In settling down in the new community, he, his wife and child must initiate a whole cluster of new (and once more temporary) relationships.

—ALVIN TOFFLER
Future Shock

Here, the main idea—that moving creates temporary relationships—is supported by the extended example of one man and his family. This single illustration is sufficiently well developed and as such it supports the topic sentence effectively.

On the other hand, several *short examples* can be employed to support an idea. Here is how this method works.

In a recent invitation to subscribe to *Ms.,* the editor, Gloria Steinem, referred to those American men who cannot understand what women want. Most women, as housewives, can seek fulfillment through their husbands and children. Working women can find their identities by satisfying their boss. Young, attractive, unmarried women realize that they can be admired as ornaments. Poor, black, and Spanish-speaking women can find satisfaction in countless ways. What, Ms. Steinem asks ironically, can the American woman possibly want when she has all these things?

Notice how these four short examples, based on four categories of women, are closely related. They are brief, but they stick to the subject. Taken together, they attack effectively the false ideas that men have about women in this country.

Application   Select one of the topic sentences that you wrote on page 147 and develop it through the use of one extended example or at least four short examples. Select your examples from personal experience, history, current events, statistics, radio, television, or film.

_____

_____

_____

_____

_____

_____

_____

_____

_____

_____

30.4. Comparison and Contrast

Comparison means the treatment of likenesses. Contrast means the treatment of differences. Sometimes you will work only with comparisons between two subjects. At other times, you will want to concentrate on contrast. Frequently you will want to use *both* comparison and contrast in developing a paragraph. Whatever strategy you choose, remember that a comparison and contrast paragraph has a very special look to it. The following are guidelines for writing the comparison and contrast paragraph.

1. *Try to concentrate on only two subjects for comparison and contrast.*

If you work with more than two, the result could be confusing.

2. *Your two subjects should be from the same category.*

It is more reasonable to compare two different car models (both are in the same category—vehicles) than it is to compare a car and an ant (each is in a different category—vehicles and insects).

3. Always state the purpose behind the comparison of two subjects.

This should be handled in your topic sentence. In other words, in your topic sentence you must explain *why* a comparison of two subjects is worthwhile. If you have decided to compare two economy cars, the Chevrolet and the Volkswagen, you might want to start with the following sentence: "A Volkswagen will always outperform a Chevrolet because of the more advanced state of German automotive skills over American methods of production." This is a topic sentence because it states your main idea; it also explains the purpose behind the comparison to test the relative merits of a foreign economy car against an American model.

4. Don't forget the need for points of comparison in a comparison and contrast paragraph.

Jot down various comparative points about your two subjects before you begin to write.

5. Organize your paragraph in one of two ways—by the block method or by the alternating method.

Information on these methods of comparison and contrast follows.

The Block Method

In the block method, you write everything about Subject A and then everything about Subject B. The effect will look like this:

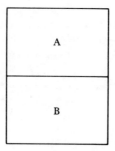

Here is a short paragraph that employs the block method.

Topic sentence establishes the two subjects, announces a contrast, and states the purpose behind the contrast. The way of the desert and the way of the jungle represent the two opposite methods of reaching stability at two extremes of density. In the jungle there is plenty of everything life needs except mere space, and it is not for want of anything else that individuals die or that races have any limit set to their proliferation. Everything is on top of everything

*All about
subject A
(the jungle)*

*Good Transition
to subject B*

*All about
subject B
(the desert)*

else; there is no cranny which is not both occupied and disputed. At every moment, war to the death rages fiercely. The place left vacant by any creature that dies is seized almost instantly by another, and life seems to suffer from nothing except too favorable an environment. In the desert, on the other hand, it is the environment itself which serves as the limiting factor. To some extent the struggle of creature against creature is mitigated, though it is of course not abolished even in the vegetable kingdom. For the plant which in the one place would be strangled to death by its neighbor dies a thirsty seedling in the desert because that same neighbor has drawn the scant moisture from the spot of earth out of which it was attempting to spring.

from JOSEPH WOOD KRUTCH
The Desert Year

In this paragraph, the writer says everything about A and then everything about B. But notice that Krutch concentrates on the vegetation and on the animal life for both the jungle and the desert. Notice also how he provides a skillful transition from A to B (see pp. 150–152 for information on transitions) and how his last sentence draws the two subjects back together.

The Alternating Method

In the alternating method of comparison and contrast, you break your two subjects into points which you deal with jointly. This approach is sometimes called the *point-by-point* method. It looks like this:

| Subject A |
| Subject B |

| Subject A |
| Subject B |

| Subject A |
| Subject B |

This alternating method of paragraph development is indicated clearly in the following paragraph.

*Note that sentences
1 and 2 actually
constitute the
topic statement.*

There are two Americas. One is the America of Lincoln and Adlai Stevenson; the other is the America of Teddy Roosevelt and the modern

Point 1
for A and B

superpatriots. One is generous and humane, the other narrowly ego-tistical; one is self-critical, the other self-righteous; one is sensible, the other romantic; one is good-humored, the other solemn; one is inquiring, the other pontificating; one is moderate, the other filled with passionate intensity; one is judicious and the other arrogant in the use of power.

Point 2
Point 3
Point 4
Point 5
Point 6

Point 7

J. WILLIAM FULBRIGHT
The Arrogance of Power

In this paragraph, Fulbright has used parallel structure effectively to keep the two subjects balanced. Note especially his use of the semicolon. Could he have used any other form of punctuation to separate items in the last long sentence?

Application 1 Write a comparative paragraph on one of the following subjects. Use either the block or alternating method of paragraph development. In addition, develop at least three specific points of comparison or contrast in your paragraph.

a. Two sports stars.

b. Two teachers you have known.

c. Two restaurants.

d. Two films or television programs.

e. Two boyfriends or girlfriends.

_____

_____

_____

_____

_____

_____

_____

_____

_____

_____

_____

_____

_____

_____

Application 2 Bring to class two photographs or illustrations that
have strong points of comparison and contrast. Be prepared to discuss
the comparative points in class.

30.5. Classification

Classification is a special form of paragraph development based on the
treatment of all important items in a category and the sorting of these
items into separate groups and subgroups. Many subjects lend themselves to classification. We talk frequently about types of college teachers,
types of music, types of cars, types of men and women. What we are
doing is classifying items within one class. This method resembles comparison and contrast. However, comparison and contrast normally involves the treatment of only two subjects in the same category, whereas
classification requires the treatment of *all* important groups in the
category.

Assume that your social science teacher wants you to write a paper on
the three branches of the Federal government. The starting point in such
an assignment involves the systematic classification and division of all
material relating to the subject.

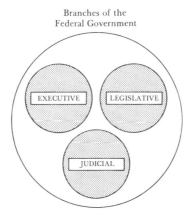

Branches of the
Federal Government

EXECUTIVE LEGISLATIVE

JUDICIAL

Although the major groups are apparent in the diagram above, you probably will have to divide (break each group into important subgroups) your material further. Essentially, complete classification results in the creation of an outline that is highly valuable in the writing process.

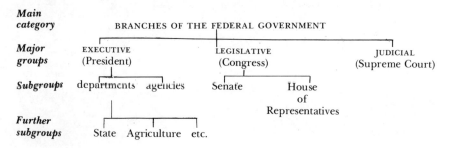

Main category   BRANCHES OF THE FEDERAL GOVERNMENT

Major groups   EXECUTIVE (President)   LEGISLATIVE (Congress)   JUDICIAL (Supreme Court)

Subgroups   departments   agencies   Senate   House of Representatives

Further subgroups   State   Agriculture   etc.

Notice that in moving from top to bottom in this outline, you are progressing from general to specific. In other words, as you move from one layer to another in a classification outline, you become more detailed in your treatment of the subject. Of course, in order to break a subject down properly, you must know something about it. If you are uncertain about the branches of government, but your instructor asks you to write something on the subject, then you have to compile information about it.

Usually it is easy to detect classification at work in a paragraph. Here is a paragraph on contraception that relies on classification.

With the availability of numerous forms of contraception, it is surprising that the danger of overpopulation still exists in the world today. We have moved beyond such simple and "natural" forms of contraception as the rhythm method, coitus interruptus, or even abstention. These methods, advocated by various religious denominations, are the least effective forms of contraception, because they depend far too much on the will power of individuals. On the other hand, there are many nonprescribed and prescribed contraceptive procedures available to people. Items that can be purchased over the counter include a variety of condoms, and also a large assortment of jellies, creams, and foams. Moreover, individuals can have doctors prescribe "pills," diaphrams, or IUD's. Finally, there are surgical procedures—vasectomies for men and the tying of the Fallopian tubes for women—that provide complete protection against conception. Because of these forms of contraception, America has now reached the stage of zero population growth. Unfortunately, with the world population soaring beyond four billion people, it is clear that other nations have not yet availed themselves of the technology of contraception.

If we were to establish a classification outline for this paragraph, we could readily identify four basic groups.

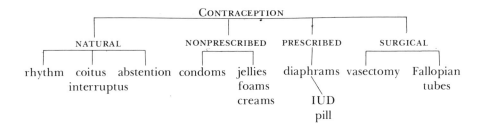

The writer of this paragraph has "read" her classification outline well. She has moved from top to bottom, and from left to right. Consequently, the paragraph has sound organization.

If you study the classification paragraph on contraception, the following guidelines for classification papers will be reflected in the material:

1. Treat all major groups in your category.
2. Make certain that you have a main idea (a topic sentence) that links these groups in a meaningful way.
3. Do not misplace items in groups. Also avoid the excessive overlapping of groups and the inclusion of material that doesn't belong in the category. For instance, you would not want to include information on IUD's under the nonprescribed form of contraception. Likewise, you have to maintain distinctions between and among categories. Finally, you would not want to discuss "test-tube" babies because this is not a valid group within the classification scheme.
4. Remember to use transitions as you move from group to group.
5. Finish with a good clincher sentence.

Classification papers are not easy to write, but the method, when mastered, does provide an excellent way to structure longer paragraphs and essays.

Application 1   Develop a classification outline for one of these topics, or for any other topic that appeals to you:

a. popular music

b. smoking

c. college men or women

d. American cars

e. sports

Application 2   Write a classification paragraph based on your outline.

_____

_____

_____

_____

_____

_____

_____

_____

_____

_____

_____

Application 3   Discuss the classification process that is evident in the following diagram provided by a major distributor of art supplies on college campuses.

Original Graphic Arts Processes: DISTRIBUTED BY FERDINAND ROTEN GALLERIES, INC.

PROCESS:	RELIEF	INTAGLIO	PLANOGRAPHIC	STENCIL
Common Name:	(A) Woodcut Linocut Embossing (B) Wood Engraving **COLLOGRAPH**	Engraving Drypoint Mezzotint Etching Aquatint	Lithograph	Serigraph (Silkscreen)
What area prints:	Prints what is left of the original surface	Prints what is below the surface of the plate	Prints what is drawn on the surface	Prints open areas of the stencil
Type of Press:	(A) Household tablespoon (B) Washington Press or Letterpress	Etching Press (Clotheswringer type)	Litho Press (Sliding, scraping pressure)	Original Serigraphs are usually hand screened
Materials:	(A) Plank-grain wood Linoleum (B) End-grain wood	Copper Zinc Plastics, etc.	Limestone Zinc Aluminum Plates, etc.	Silk Organdie Nylon, etc.
Basic Tools:	Knife Gouge Burin, etc.	Etching Needles Burins Acids Grounds, etc.	Litho Crayon Tusche Litho Rubbing Ink, etc.	Squeegee Screen Nufilm Glue Tusche, etc.

(© American Home Publishing Company, Inc.).

30.6. Definition

There are two kinds of definition: the *short definition* (or dictionary definition), which is useful to briefly identify a term for the reader, and the *extended definition,* which is a pattern of explanation that might involve a paragraph or an entire essay. Definitions, whether they are short or extended, are important in producing clear writing; as such, they are key features of many forms of paragraphs.

> *Hint:* Do not begin a paragraph with a simple dictionary definition, or with such hackneyed expressions as "Webster's dictionary states," or "According to my dictionary." Invent more sophisticated ways to present dictionary definitions.

In an absorbing book entitled *Whales and Men,* the author, R. B. Robertson, provides an interesting extended definition of the blue whale:

In describing whales, and especially that greatest of them all—*Sibbaldus musculus,* the blue whale, or sulphur-bottom—one quickly runs out of adjectives, or, rather, never finds a single adequate one. Huge, immense, enormous, titanic, mighty, vast, stupendous, monstrous, gigantic, elephantine, colossal, Cyclopean, Gargantuan—these are about the only adjectives that Roget can find to help, and not only are they all incapable of conveying an idea of the bulk of the blue whale to a person who has never seen one but some are downright misleading. "Elephantine," for instance, is a pygmy adjective, giving an utterly false impression of this greatest of all monsters of all time, for the blue whale has the bulk and weight of fifty elephants. Like most people, I imagine, I had always mentally accepted the fact that a whale is big, but I had never realized how its bigness transcended adjectives until I saw one close at hand three years ago, when I spent eight months serving as senior medical officer on a British whaling factory ship in the antarctic. A whaling factory ship is a hulking brute of a vessel, four hundred or more feet long, with a gaping tunnel, or skidway, leading from open water at the stern to a spacious deck area amidships, and when I saw my first blue whale—nearly a quarter as long as the ship itself—being dragged up that skidway in order to be stripped, or flensed, of its blubber on the open deck, it became clear that no word in Roget's section on bigness would ever mean the same to me again.

Notice that instead of providing a simple dictionary definition, Robertson utilizes a list of synonyms drawn from Roget's *Thesaurus.* He introduces us first to the class (or *genus*) under investigation and then to one member of the class—the blue whale. Moreover, he relies on one of the most common ways to define an object, which is *description.* Robertson also uses comparisons and personal narrative to define the blue whale. In this extended definition, there are several other forms of paragraph development at work.

Here are several ways to develop extended definitions, although you probably will not want to use all these methods in the same paragraph. Select those strategies that are most useful for your purpose.

1. Start with a question and then give the answer. In other words, begin a paragraph with questions like these:

What is socialism?
What is rhythm and blues?

Then answer the question in a careful and well-organized way.

2. Provide a description—as did Robertson—of the object that you want to define. This strategy works better for concrete objects like whales than for abstractions like "wisdom."

3. Use an *analogy* to create an extended definition. An analogy is a form of comparison in which you take a difficult idea and make it easier to understand by relating it to something the reader knows about. Suppose you want to define "creativity." An analogy must look like this: "Creativity is a lot like daydreaming." From here, you would go on to explain the impulses behind daydreaming (which we all do) in order to reveal the nature of creativity.

4. Define a term by showing what it is *not*. For instance, if you are discussing the hyena, you might begin by writing, "The hyena is not the monstrous animal that most of us imagine." You would then expand this "negative" definition by dealing with other misunderstandings about the hyena: that it is murderous, filthy, unloving, and a "loner." As a clincher, your last sentences should properly define the true nature of the hyena.

5. Simply list the characteristics of an item. You could define sports car by listing things like size, weight, engine, and seating capacity.

6. Tell a story to help define a subject. You might want to define *"juvenile offender"* by relating an incident about someone you know or have heard about who could be described as such.

Application   Write a one-paragraph extended definition for one of the following terms: soul food, beauty, juvenile offender, freedom, ghetto.

_____

_____

_____

_____

_____

_____

_____

_____

_____

_____

_____

_____

_____

_____

30.7. Analysis

Quite often in college courses you are asked to *analyze* an event, a process, a cause or effect, a work of literature or art. Basically, you are being asked to think about the subject, to examine it carefully, and to dissect it. With analysis, you cannot simply tell a story, summarize an event, or describe an object. Instead, you must explain the how and why of a topic. There are the two basic ways to perform this task.

1. *Use analysis to explain the why of things and events.*

With analysis, you can seek causes and understand effects. In the following paragraph, the student uses such analysis to explain the lives of her parents.

Why did they come?	My parents came to New York with the dream of saving enough money to return to Puerto Rico and buy a house with some land
Analysis of typical effects	and fruit trees. Many Puerto Ricans, troubled by the problem of slum life on the island, find no relief in migration to New York. They remain poor, stay in the *barrio,* are unable to cope with
Exception to common effect	American society and ways of life, and experience the destruction of their traditionally close family life. My parents were fortunate.
Personal application	After spending most of their lives working hard in the tenements of New York, they saved enough to return to the island. Today they tend their orange, lemon, banana, and plantain trees in an
Clincher sentence	area of Puerto Rico called "El Paraíso." It took them most of a lifetime to find their paradise—in their own backyard.

The student who wrote this paragraph blends personal narrative with a more objective analysis of causes and effects. Other paragraph patterns—notably comparison and contrast—aid her in developing the paragraph.

2. *Use analysis to explain the how of a subject.*

This type of analysis examines the way things are put together or how things happen. It also deals with *process:* how an automobile engine operates; how to hit a backhand shot in tennis; how to apply for a loan; how to make wine at home. Process analysis involves step-by-step procedures, as the following paragraph suggests.

If you are inexperienced in relaxation techniques, begin by sitting in a comfortable chair with your feet on the floor and your hands resting easily in your lap. Close your eyes and breathe evenly, deeply, and gently. As you exhale each breath let your body become more relaxed. Starting with one hand direct your attention to one part of your body at a time. Close your fist and tighten the muscles in your forearm. Feel the sensation of tension in your muscles. Relax your hand and let your forearm and hand become completely limp. Direct all your attention to the sensation of relaxation as you continue to let all tension leave your hand and arm. Continue this practice once or several times each day, relaxing your other hand and arm, your legs, back, abdomen, chest, neck, face, and scalp. When you have this mastered and can relax completely, turn your thoughts to scenes of peaceful beauty. Begin, if you wish, by recalling pleasant scenes of natural tranquillity from your past. Stay with your inner self as long as you wish, either thinking of nothing or visualizing only the loveliest of images. Often you will become completely unaware of your surroundings. When you open your eyes you will find yourself refreshed in mind and body.

DR. LAURENCE J. PETER

The Peter Prescription

In process analysis, begin at the start of the activity and move systemmatically through it to the conclusion.

Application 1 Write a paragraph in which you analyze *why* a personal experience turned out the way it did.

_____

_____

_____

_____

_____

_____

_____

_____

_____

_____

Application 2   Write a brief paragraph in which you analyze the *how* of a specific process or activity.

_____

_____

_____

_____

_____

_____

_____

_____

_____

_____

CHAPTER 31

The Shape of the Essay

An essay is a composition consisting of more than one paragraph. For relatively short papers of 250 to 500 words, anywhere from three to five paragraphs will be adequate for the topic. Here is how a short essay should be organized.

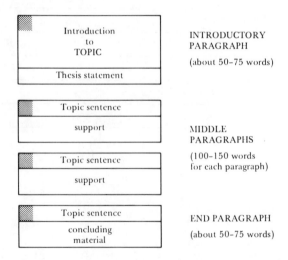

A well-organized essay will have a beginning, middle, and end. The beginning paragraph introduces the reader to the subject of the essay. It should contain a *thesis statement,* which is a one-sentence presentation of the main subject of the essay. It is more inclusive than the topic sentences in the middle paragraphs and actually embraces the ideas in the topic sentences. The thesis statement can come at the beginning of the introductory paragraph or at the end of it. Often the thesis sentence grows out of the introductory paragraph without being stated exactly in any one sentence. As with topic sentences, it is useful for writers to provide clearly defined thesis sentences.

The middle paragraphs (which compose the body of the essay) develop carefully a few major ideas that are related to the thesis statement. For each major idea (signaled by a topic sentence), you should develop a separate paragraph. Finally, the end paragraph will bring your essay to an effective conclusion. Thus each of the three primary parts of an essay has a special function or purpose, and all three parts are needed to create a balanced composition.

In writing essays, you should employ many of the devices that you have mastered already in this part of the *Handbook*. Remember that the rules for paragraph organization apply equally well to essay organization, and that such patterns as description, comparison and contrast, and analysis are integral aspects of essay form. In fact, an essay is like a long, complex paragraph that has been divided into short units for easier and better understanding.

The following selection from *Understanding English* by Paul Roberts illustrates the shape of a four-paragraph essay.

The history of English since 1700 is filled with many movements and counter-movements, of which we can notice only a couple. One of these is the vigorous attempt made in the eighteenth century, and the rather half-hearted attempts made since, to regulate and control the English language. Many people of the eighteenth century, not understanding very well the forces which govern language, proposed to polish and prune and restrict English, which they felt was proliferating too wildly. There was much talk of an academy which would rule on what people could and could not say and write. The academy never came into being, but the eighteenth century did succeed in establishing certain attitudes which, though they haven't had much effect on the development of the language itself, have certainly changed the native speaker's feeling about the language.

In part a product of the wish to fix and establish the language was the development of the dictionary. The first English dictionary was published in 1603; it was a list of 2500 words briefly defined. Many others were published with gradual improvements until Samuel Johnson published his *English Dictionary* in 1755. This, steadily revised, dominated the field in England for nearly a hundred years. Meanwhile in America, Noah Webster published his dictionary in 1828, and before long dictionary publishing was a big business in this country. The last century has seen the publication of one great dictionary: the twelve-volume *Oxford English Dictionary*, compiled in the course of seventy-five years through the labors of many scholars. We have also, of course, numerous commercial dictionaries which are as good as the public wants them to be if not, indeed, rather better.

Another product of the eighteenth century was the invention of "English grammar." As English came to replace Latin as the language of scholarship it was felt that one should also be able to control and dissect it, parse and analyze it, as one could Latin. What happened in practice was that the grammatical description that applied to Latin was removed and superimposed on English. This was silly, because English is an entirely different kind of language, with its own forms and signals and ways of producing meaning. Nevertheless, English grammars on the Latin model were worked out and taught in the schools. In many schools they are still being taught. This activity is not often popular with school children, but it is sometimes an interesting and instructive exercise in logic. The principal harm in it is that it has tended to keep people from being interested in English and has obscured the real features of English structure.

But probably the most important force on the development of English in the modern period has been the tremendous expansion of English-speaking peoples. In 1500 English was a minor language, spoken by a few people on a small island. Now it is perhaps the greatest language of the world, spoken natively by over a quarter of a billion people and as a second language by many millions more. When we speak of English now, we must specify whether we mean American English, British English, Australian English, Indian English, or what, since the differences are considerable. The American cannot go to England or the Englishman to America confident that he will always understand and be understood. The Alabaman in Iowa or the Iowan in Alabama shows himself a foreigner every time he speaks. It is only because communication has become fast and easy that English in this period of its expansion has not broken into a dozen mutually unintelligible languages.

This essay runs to approximately 600 words—a length expected of students in many composition courses. Roberts, of course, knows his subject, and consequently he writes about it easily. Moreover, he designs his essay around a clear beginning, a well-developed middle section, and a solid conclusion. The main topics emerge clearly from this essay because of the careful way in which Roberts has shaped his materials.

Application 1   Answer the following questions about Roberts' essay.

a. Roberts' thesis statement actually consists of two sentences—the first and last ones in the introductory paragraph. Why is this an effective strategy? _____

_____

b. What are the topic sentences for paragraphs two, three, and four?

Paragraph 2 _____

_____

Paragraph 3 _____

_____

Paragraph 4 _____

_____

How are these topics related to the thesis statement? _____

_____

c. How does Roberts achieve coherence in this essay? _____

_____

d. Where does Roberts use comparison and contrast as a pattern for his paragraph? What are the subjects of the comparison? _____

_____

e. This essay is strong in its use of examples. What paragraph makes use of a series of short, related examples? Are there any extended examples in the essay? _____

_____

_____

Application 2   If you have written long, single-paragraph compositions, you probably have developed enough material in such papers to turn the paragraph into an essay. In fact, a very long paragraph, because of the wealth of information that it contains, should be divided into smaller units. These smaller units, paragraphs in themselves, will permit the reader to grasp information more readily. Examine the following paragraph that was written by a student and then work with it according to the directions provided.

HICKS

Anyone who has grown up exclusively in an urban area would find it impossible to judge city and country life objectively. I have been a city resident all my life. But I had the good fortune to be able to spend a summer in the mountains of eastern Pennsylvania. Because of this experience I had to redefine my notion of the American hick. Perhaps from reading too many books and seeing too many films about "hillbillies" and "rednecks," I expected negative encounters with the natives. To my surprise, all of my pre-established notions went down the drain after just a few short days. The people were very warm and friendly and did not consider me as an outsider—a person not to be trusted yet. They even seemed to go out of their way to compensate for my ignorance of country living. One of the things I particularly got satisfaction from in the country was the lack of preoccupation with clothing styles and with the need to be "cool." Walking around with a three-day growth of beard and not getting dirty looks was a vacation in itself. When I returned to the city and walked down my block. I tried to imagine what it would be like for a country person in my neighborhood. He probably would experience stares from many eyes—some suspicious, some with an innocent curiosity, some bold and filled with laughter over his clothes and manner of speech. In some of the more ethnocentric neighborhoods, he would certainly be unable to forget his being different, perhaps through self-consciousness but more likely by the attitudes of the people. These experiences go a long way in redefining my own image of what a "hick" is. Someone who is so wrapped up in the provinciality and idiosyncrasies of his own way of life that anyone from outside is approached defensively is the true hick. It's the tough city streets like mine that make us into urban hicks. We have it all over our country cousins.

a. *Thesis Statement:* Identify the central idea in this theme by underlining it twice. If you think that more than one sentence is involved in the thesis statement, use double underlines for all material that is relevant.

b. *Paragraph to Essay:* Try to break this theme into four segments consisting of an opening paragraph, two middle paragraphs, and an ending paragraph. Underline the topic sentences for paragraphs two, three, and four.

c. *Understanding Patterns:* Which methods of paragraph and essay development does the writer use in this theme? In other words, does he use narration, comparison and contrast, classification, or what? How do these patterns serve as guides to the division of the theme into an essay?

d. *Making the Change:* Rewrite this piece in essay form. Don't forget to indent each new paragraph. Rewrite material if you want. You should also have a minimum of three sentences in each paragraph.

CHAPTER 32

Planning the Essay: The Outline

Because the essay involves a more complicated organizational plan than the single-paragraph composition, it is worthwhile to develop an *outline* before you start writing. An outline is a "frame" for your essay. It requires you to organize your main ideas around a central thesis and to design a beginning, middle, and end for your essay. It also forces you to establish supporting ideas for your main ideas—to determine the relative importance of the material that you plan to use in the essay. Outlines exist in several forms or designs. A typical scratch outline appears below. Familiarize yourself with the conventional symbols used and the way in which material is indented to indicate its relative weight or significance within the essay.

MY SISTER DOLORES

Thesis statement: My sister Dolores is a real nut, as evidenced by her behavior at our block party last summer.

   I. The appearance of Dolores.
      A. Her dress and looks.
         1. Matching slacks and shoes.
         2. Hair, earrings, and makeup.
      B. Her initial behavior.
         1. Her prancing.
         2. Her shouting.
  II. Dolores as the life of the party.
      A. Her jokes.
      B. Her "act."
      C. The sermon.
 III. The climax of the day.
      A. The races start.
      B. Dolores breaks them up.

Conclusion: I was terribly embarrassed by Dolores' behavior, but the block wants her back for next year's party.

Hint: The thesis statement and the conclusion are not parts of the outline. However, because they serve as the beginning and end of the projected essay, they should appear as complete sentences framing the outline.

An outline, whether it is composed of sentences, phrases, or single words, helps to plan an essay. Of course, the more detailed you make it (in terms of the amount of supporting evidence listed for each main division), the easier the writing of the essay will be. If you want, jot down fifteen or twenty ideas about your subject and then divide them according to the demands of the outline for major and minor points. If you have general divisions in mind already, you might begin with the outline itself. Outlines are not needed by all writers. However, if an essay seems like an unmanageable creature to you, an outline can be of value.

Application 1 Here is the student's essay based on the sample outline provided in this section. Answer the questions that follow it.

MY SISTER DOLORES

My younger sister Dolores, who is often referred to as being crazy or a real nut, still has people talking about her antics at the annual block party last summer. How vividly I recall the day Dolores and her husband arrived with their four children in their old Dodge car. It was around noon. Cheers from the rest of the family in my front yard rang out as they recognized the car. "Now the party begins!" someone shouted.

Dolores emerged from the car in a beautiful two-piece kelly green slack outfit. Her shoes were of the same color. Her long hair hung neatly down to her shoulders. Silver hoop earrings graced her ears and sparkled like diamonds in the bright sunshine. Her makeup made her face look like a beautiful bronze doll. Dolores was truly a sight to behold as she pranced around in a haughty manner. "What you see is what you'd like to get," she shouted to the man hanging the banners. He responded with a toothless grin and almost fell off the ladder.

Soon, everyone was laughing heartily at the many jokes Dolores told. Before long, a crowd gathered at my front gate. Dolores excused herself, saying she would be right back. She came out of my house wearing a large lounging gown that hung halfway down her legs. As she sat down, she raised the gown and revealed a pair of men's argyle knee socks. On her feet were my husband's old combat boots. I didn't know whether to laugh or find a hole to crawl into, as my minister had since arrived and was sitting in my yard. The crowd roared their approval and Dolores went into her act, doing all kinds of crazy dances in this weird outfit. The minister got ready to leave and asked us to join him in a moment of prayer. Right in the middle of the prayer a loud "Amen" rang out. I winced as I recognized Dolores' voice. There were smothered giggles throughout the crowd. I vowed never to return to my church again.

The races were beginning and the children were all excited, as trophies were given to the winners. Then it was time for the final big race. Big boys had practiced for weeks for this event, as a large, beautiful trophy would go to the winner. The whistle blew and the boys darted out at a fast pace. I cheered loudly as my son Richie ran past me leading all the others. All of a sudden, from out of the crowd a splash of color was next to Richie. Oh, no. It was Dolores running next to Richie, combat boots and all. My son won as the other runners laughed hysterically and could run no farther. The finale was when Dolores reached the finish line, took off her hair and handed it to one of the judges, saying, "Hold this a minute, I have to catch my breath."

It took me two weeks to face that neighbor. I didn't know how to explain Dolores. Now it's time again for the annual block party and I am besieged by my neighbors, asking if Dolores will come again this year. "We won't have any fun unless she comes," they say. I must make my decision soon. Can you guess what it will be?

a. What are some of the relationships between the outline and the essay?

b. Does the writer have a clearly identified topic sentence for each paragraph, or does she employ other strategies to hold paragraphs together? What does this say about the nature of the topic sentence?

c. How many sentences are in the opening and ending paragraphs? What does this suggest about the introductory and concluding paragraphs in relationship to the body of the essay?

d. Does each paragraph in the body of the essay deal with one topic or with a set of related topics? Why is it necessary to have a specific focus in each paragraph?

e. How does the writer connect all the paragraphs so that there are no breaks in the essay? Would you say that transitions are even more important in essays than in single paragraphs?

Application 2　Select a topic (quite possibly one of the topic sentences you earlier will be helpful) and then prepare an outline for a four- to five-paragraph essay. Feel free to write complete sentences, or use "scratch" phrases like the author of the essay on Dolores did. For now, do *not* write an essay based on this outline.

Outline

CHAPTER 33

The Introductory Paragraph

Now that you have developed an outline for your essay, you should turn your attention to the introductory paragraph. As you know, the introductory paragraph is the beginning part of the essay. As such, it must do three things:

1. introduce the topic
2. limit the topic
3. make the reader interested in the topic

Primarily you have to "hook" the reader. Otherwise he or she will not be interested in your topic. There are ways to create this quick interest.

First of all, *make the introductory paragraph short.* Introduce the subject and limit it with a good thesis or proposal sentence. Don't waste words. Usually three to seven sentences will make a good introductory paragraph.

Second, don't apologize for the quality of your writing. Similarly, don't apologize for your lack of knowledge of the subject. First sentences like "I really don't know much about American Indians, so this essay is bound to be weak" will assuredly disturb a reader.

Finally, avoid any mechanical explanation of how the essay will develop. Don't give the reader your outline in the opening paragraph (although you *can* include references to your main topics). What you should stay away from are rigid sentences that create a "first I will do this and then I will do that" effect. This makes for stiff and uninteresting introductions.

In addition to these general guidelines, there are specific ways not only to make your introductory paragraph appealing but also to develop it fully. Some of these special strategies are given below. Quite frequently you will be able to combine some of these methods in the introductory paragraph.

Ten tips for developing introductory paragraphs

1. Simply state the importance of your topic as strongly as possible.
2. State your subject and give some useful examples that you plan to pursue in the body of your essay.
3. Ask a question or series of questions that relate to your topic.
4. Begin with a brief story that sets the stage for your topic.
5. Begin with a quotation that reveals an important part of your topic.
6. Use vivid description to support your topic.
7. Present startling facts, figures, or statistics that bear on your subject.
8. Refer to an historic event or series of events to set up your topic.
9. Use a point of comparison or contrast to introduce your topic.
10. Explain that what many people believe is true about your subject will be proven false in your essay.

Application 1   Read the sample introductory paragraph that appears below and then answer the questions that follow it.

How many times have we heard the expression, "My country, right or wrong"? Historically we have used the phrase to defend the elimination of the American Indian, the taking of land from Mexico, the bombing of Hiroshima and Nagasaki. More recently we have invoked it to explain the sacrifice of 50,000 young Americans and the expenditure of more than $125 billion in Vietnam. Moreover, for a long time a majority of Americans failed to find dishonor in Watergate. It is easy to subscribe to popular phrases, but truly patriotic Americans will know when their country is wrong and will not try to find honor in dishonor.

a. Which sentence serves as the thesis statement in this introductory paragraph?_____

b. How many of the tips for developing topic sentences did the writer include in this paragraph? Which ones are they? _____

_____

_____

c. Does the writer succeed in arousing your interest?_____

_____

d. Do you think that you have been prepared for what might follow in the middle paragraphs of this essay? In what way? _____

_____

e. Do you think that the writer will be able to move smoothly into the next paragraph of the essay? Why or why not? _____

_____

Application 2   Return to your essay outline on page 184. Look at the thesis statement. Also reread the Ten Tips for Developing Introductory Paragraphs. Then write an effective introductory paragraph for your essay.

_____

_____

_____

_____

_____

_____

_____

_____

CHAPTER 34

The Middle Paragraphs: Building from the Introduction

The middle part or body of your essay is usually the longest section in your paper. It may consist of a single paragraph or a series of paragraphs. In either case, the purpose of these middle paragraphs is to develop the main idea (the thesis sentence) presented in the introductory paragraph. The middle paragraphs present facts, details, arguments, and explanations supporting the thesis sentence.

The function of your middle paragraphs is not to develop a series of minor ideas, but rather to develop a few main subtopics that relate to the thesis statement. Thus it is often useful to have one topic sentence for each paragraph in the body of the essay, and to place that topic sentence at the start of the paragraph. Of course, in some middle paragraphs—especially paragraphs involving narration and description—there is no need for a clearly identifiable topic sentence; in such middle paragraphs, blocks in time and space permit a certain unity of effect.

In striving for the best effect and the clearest meaning in middle paragraphs, you have to make choices in determining what pattern of development is best for your subject. The best choices available to you correspond to information already presented on organizing paragraphs through patterns (see pp. 157–176). Select the pattern or patterns that will permit you to develop the thesis sentence most effectively.

Tips for developing middle paragraphs

1. *Develop middle paragraphs chronologically.* Start at a certain point in time and progress in stages, with each major block of time set in a paragraph of its own.
2. *Develop middle paragraphs spatially.* Describe people, places, and things (which exist in space) in an orderly manner—from top to bottom, far away to near, general to particular.

3. *Develop middle paragraphs through comparison and contrast.* Use either the block or alternating method (see pp. 163–167) to present key points of comparison and contrast.
4. *Develop middle paragraphs through classification.* If your subject lends itself division into categories (groups and sub-groups), write a paragraph for each of the major categories in that subject.
5. *Develop middle paragraphs through process analysis.* Follow a process clearly through successive stages. Employ strict chronological order, remembering to include all important steps in the process. If your process is lengthy or technical, break it up into manageable paragraphs.

As you move into the body of the essay, create an effective *transition* (see pp. 150–152) from the introductory to the middle paragraph. Transitions are needed inside paragraphs and also between paragraphs in order to have a coherent essay. You can establish a good transition from the introductory to the middle paragraph by positioning the thesis sentence properly, by repeating a key idea mentioned in the introductory paragraph, or simply starting the body with the most obvious supporting idea that grows out of the introduction.

> *Hint:* A thesis statement that has been placed at the end of the introductory paragraph can serve as a good lead into the body of the essay.

The student paragraph in the exercise on page 186 reflects these techniques. Transitions from paragraph to paragraph in the body of the student's essay were based on material presented in the introductory paragraph.

Ending Paragraph 1   It is easy to subscribe to popular phrases, but truly patriotic Americans will know when their country is wrong and will not try to find honor in dishonor.

Starting Paragraph 2   Increasing numbers of truly patriotic Americans started to question our involvement in Vietnam in the 1960's.

Starting Paragraph 3   Another crisis that tested Americans understanding of patriotism was the Watergate affair.

Here, there is clear progression from thesis statement, to topic sentence 1, and to topic sentence 2.

Many of the most successful middle paragraphs in an essay start with topic sentences. Of course, within each middle paragraph you also have to arrange information in an orderly and convincing manner. By starting with a topic sentence, you are presenting the most important information first; you should then move to other important details, and finally to less important details. This procedure can be found in a great deal of newspaper writing, and it can be applied properly in your own essays. The procedure can be diagrammed again in terms of the inverted triangle:

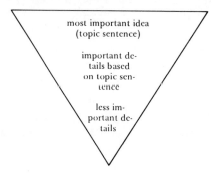

Try to order the information in your middle paragraphs in this manner.

Application 1   Read the paragraph below and then answer the questions that follow it.

The hazardous conditions were supposedly compensated for by high wages. Auto workers were among the highest paid workers in the United States, yet wage scales were deceptive. In the 1920's, Henry Ford made headlines by promising $5.00 a day to every worker in his enterprises. Ford workers soon discovered that it was not quite $5.00 a day for not quite everyone. Fully a third of all Ford workers never got the $5.00 a day. Likewise, at Eldon, the 1969 $4.00 an hour average Chrysler wage proved a fiction. Before any deductions and without the cost of living factor, which did not cover all workers and was never more than 21¢ an hour, most job categories at Eldon paid around $3.60 an hour and none paid more than $3.94 to workers.

DAN GEORGAKAS AND MARVIN SURKIN
Detroit: I Do Mind Dying

a. How can you tell that this is a middle paragraph rather than an
opening or ending paragraph?_____ _____

_____

b. What is the main idea in this paragraph? _____

_____

c. What is the topic sentence in this paragraph?_____

_____

d. How do the writers develop the paragraph?_____

_____

e. Do all the facts presented in the paragraph relate to the topic? Are the facts presented in a well-organized way?_____

_____

Application 2 Write the middle paragraphs for the essay outline that you developed earlier on page 184. Check the introductory paragraph already written so that you can create a good link between the beginning and middle units in the essay.

_____

_____

_____

_____

_____

_____

_____

_____

_____

_____

_____

_____

_____

_____

_____

_____

_____

_____

_____

_____

_____

_____

_____

CHAPTER 35

The Closing Paragraph: How to End the Essay

All essays require a *closing* paragraph—a paragraph designed to wrap things up, to provide a finishing touch, and to satisfy our expectation for completeness. The function of the closing paragraph is simply to conclude the essay. Yet closing paragraphs are probably the most difficult to write; they are also the ones that college students most frequently overlook.

Here are some hints for creating good end paragraphs.

1. Merely summarize the main points in your essay. If your essay is short, however, you run the risk of repetition. A summary paragraph is more effective in longer essays and in research papers.
2. Use techniques like questions and quotations that were suggested for closing sentences in paragraphs. (See pp. 154–155.)
3. Have the end paragraph serve as a climax. This is especially effective in narrative writing.
4. Pose possible solutions to the problems and issues that you raised in your essay.
5. Come back to some significant aspect of your introductory paragraph and add to it. This creates a roundness of effect—almost as if the essay has come full circle.
6. Restate only the main idea (the thesis statement), but add related observations to it so that its full significance is revealed.

As with the introductory paragraph, there are certain things that you should *not* do in an end paragraph. Do not apologize, complain, contradict your main point, add an afterthought, or raise an additional point that should have gone in the middle of the essay. Finally, try to keep the conclusion short, but not *too* short: a one- or two-sentence ending is rarely effective.

Essay

Application Write the conclusion for the essay which you have been working on in this section.

_____

_____

_____

_____

_____

_____

CHAPTER 36

Revising the Essay

Before submitting an essay, you should make certain that everything is in order. Quite frequently, it is useful to rework material, to add information, or to take out items that do not contribute to the quality of the essay. This process of checking and adjusting, of adding and eliminating, is called *revision*. In order to make the process of revision successful, you should try to answer the questions that are outlined below.

ESSAY CHECKLIST

1. TITLE
   a. Have you given your essay a title? All essays (and also single paragraph themes) should have a title.
   b. Have your capitalized all necessary words in the title? (See the section on capitalization, pp. 132–134.)
   c. Does the title reveal the subject of the essay?
   d. Does the title capture the reader's interest?
   e. Is the title short and to the point? (Try to avoid long titles; also avoid complete sentences for titles.)

2. BEGINNING PARAGRAPH
   a. Does the opening paragraph *establish* and *limit* the topic?
   b. Is the purpose or intention of the essay (expressed by a thesis sentence) clear?
   c. Do you use the right devices to gain reader interest? (See p. 186.)
   d. Is the beginning paragraph of the right length?
   e. Do you prepare the reader for a smooth transition into the middle of the essay?
   f. Are all sentences grammatically correct? Do you vary your sentences successfully? Are there transitions from sentence to sentence?

3. MIDDLE PARAGRAPHS
   a. Do you have a topic sentence (one main idea) for each paragraph in the middle (or body) of the essay?

b. Does each sentence help to develop or support the topic sentence?

c. Is there enough support for the topic sentence?

d. Are there smooth transitions within each paragraph and between paragraphs?

e. Are your sentences grammatically correct, varied in length, and ordered properly?

4. END PARAGRAPH

a. Do you leave the reader with the feeling that your last paragraph successfully wraps up the essay?

b. Have the right devices been used to make the end paragraph successful? (See p. 193.)

c. Are all sentences correct and appropriate?

Application 1 On a separate sheet of paper, write the entire essay which you have been working on in this section. Make any necessary revisions suggested by the Essay Checklist. Also make certain that the form of the essay (see pp. 252–253) is acceptable.

PART 4

Effective Writing for Courses and Jobs

In this part of the *Handbook* you will find essential information that will help you to design research papers; write effectively about literature, the social sciences, science, and business; compose solid responses to examination questions; and prepare papers for submission to class instructors. The section on business writing has a special relevance because it prepares you for a variety of work situations where a knowledge of business English is critical to your success. In all sections, you will discover that the process of writing well is more than an art that any educated person can take pride in. Good writing is also needed for survival. You cannot afford to neglect it.

CHAPTER 37

The Short
Research Paper

A research paper is a special type of essay. It is an essay that includes information that you have obtained from other sources. Typical sources are newspapers, magazines, books, and encyclopedias. The best place to find all these sources together is in a library. Therefore, you will usually have to do some work in the library in order to write a good research paper.

You must locate information in the library, take the information down in note form, arrange it, and document it properly when you write a research paper. Documentation involves the use of footnotes and a bibliography. Footnotes direct the reader to the exact source of your information. A bibliography usually lists all the works that you have found about your topic, even if you have not used information from all of them for your paper.

In all research papers there is a need to balance your "found" information with your own ideas. You might agree or disagree with the writer of an article or book that you have used. Or a quotation that you put in your research paper might suggest an insight of your own. In short, never rely exclusively on your found information. A good research paper will always reveal your own ideas and the attitudes of others as well.

Of course, a solid research paper will reflect all the rules of writing, development, and organization treated in earlier sections of this text. At the same time, a research paper builds on these rules and adds to them. A research paper involves clear steps in preparation and a special attention to the details of documenting facts. The steps and details essential to writing a solid research paper appear in this section.

37.1. Steps in Writing the Research Paper

Before you write a research paper, you must prepare for it. This is as true of a short research paper of four or five pages as it is of a long term paper of twenty pages. If you follow these steps, your research paper should be successful.

1. *Choose a topic carefully.*

First, the topic should be of interest to you; if it is, the chances are that you already know something about it and that you might even have read something about it. Second, you should have a feeling that there is enough material available on your topic; this will make the research effort easier. Third, you should choose a topic that will permit you to form your own ideas about it. For example, it is hard to form an opinion about the development of the Xerox machine. It is easier to form an opinion about the dropping of the atom bomb on Hiroshima during World War Two. Therefore, a paper about the dropping of the atom bomb would permit you to balance research findings with your own ideas.

2. *Have a general plan to limit your topic.*

In other words, you must fit the topic of the demands of the assignment. You cannot risk being too broad or general in your selection of a topic. The movement from general to specific, which has been discussed earlier, applies to the limitation of the topic in research papers. This movement, as you recall, resembles a triangle that has been turned upside down. Look at the following diagram to see again how the method works.

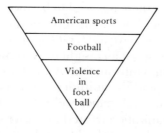

3. *Develop a list of works to read for information.*

Once you know your topic, you should go to the library *card catalogue* and to various *indexes* for information. The library card catalogue actually consists of three files; these files list information about a book in terms of author, title, and subject. In other words, you have an author catalogue, title catalogue, and subject catalogue for reference purposes. Of the three, the subject catalogue is the best place to start your research. As with author and title catalogues, everything is listed alphabetically in a subject catalogue. A typical entry in the subject catalogue will look like this:

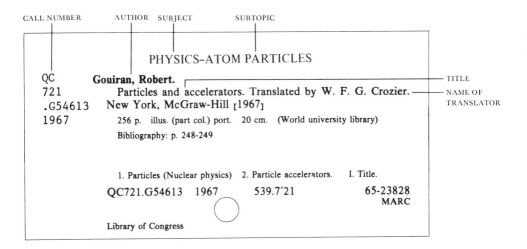

CALL NUMBER   AUTHOR SUBJECT   SUBTOPIC

PHYSICS–ATOM PARTICLES

QC   **Gouiran, Robert.**   TITLE
721   Particles and accelerators. Translated by **W. F. G. Crozier.**   NAME OF
.G54613   New York, McGraw-Hill [1967]   TRANSLATOR
1967   256 p.   illus. (part col.) port.   20 cm.   (World university library)
                  Bibliography: p. 248-249

                  1. Particles (Nuclear physics)   2. Particle accelerators.   I. Title.
                  QC721.G54613   1967   539.7'21   65-23828
                                                                        MARC

            Library of Congress

Check as many subjects that might be related to your topic as possible. Let's say that you are interested in city planning. In addition to "cities" and "towns," what other subjects might you check? Again, if you were writing a paper about the atom bomb and Hiroshima, what subjects would you look under for source material?

The second major source for listings on your topic are indexes. Indexes list magazine and newspaper articles on a given subject. Most major indexes in a library list material by subject. Such indexes usually are kept in a special library reference section. Ask your librarian for help in locating the following indexes for possible use in researching your topic.

1. *Readers' Guide to Periodical Literature.* This is the main index to use in researching your subject. It contains information about articles published in popular magazines in this country. Perhaps you want to do a paper on the condition of nursing homes in America. In the *Reader's Guide to Periodical Literature,* you will find information on your subject similar to that in the illustration on the next page.[1] tration below.
2. *Book Review Digest:* an index to reviews of books in many fields.
3. *Business Periodicals Index:* a subject index to articles in business areas.
4. *Education Index:* an index listing articles on education.
5. *New York Times Index:* lists articles published in *The New York Times.*
6. *Newsbank Index:* an index to articles on urban problems.
7. *Social Sciences Index* and *Humanities Index:* list articles of a scholarly nature in the humanities and the social sciences.

[1] *Readers' Guide to Periodical Literature* Copyright © 1971, 1972. Material reproduced by permission of The H. W. Wilson Company.

NUREEV, Rudolf—*Continued*
Rehearsal. J. Pikula. il por Dance Mag 48:
13 D '74 •
Taylor made; dance debut in Aureole with
the Paul Taylor dance company. J. Nuch-
tern. il Dance Mag 48:73-5 D '74 •
NURSE midwives. See Midwives
NURSERIES (horticulture)
Exploring western Sonoma County's unusual
nurseries. il Sunset 153:134-5 Ag '74
New England's organic-minded nurseries. M.
C. Goldman. il Org Gard & Farm 21:96-101
O '74
See also
American garden products, inc
NURSERIES, Day. See Day nurseries
NURSERY schools
How to start a co-op nursery school. G. M.
Knox. il Bet Hom & Gard 52:68+ My '74
See also
Play schools
NURSES and nursing
See also
School nurses
NURSES and patients
Extreme mercy. L. E. Sissman. Atlantic 235:
16+ Ja '75
NURSES dormitories. See Dormitories
NURSING (infant feeding) See Breast feeding
NURSING homes
Elizabeth Addison goes home. M. Kellogg. il
McCalls 101:106-7+ My '74
Exploiting the aged; investigation by Mary
Adelaide Mendelson. Time 103:69+ Je 3 '74
Many nursing home residents needn't be
there, study shows. Aging 233:14 Mr '74
Pennsylvania to move aged from substandard
care homes. Aging 233:13 Mr '74
Political economy of nursing homes. M. A.
Mendelson and D. Hapgood. Ann Am Acad
415:95-105 S '74
Salem city sets up for low cost extended care;
Salem, Mass. long-term care facility. il
Archit Rec 156:141 Ag '74
Tender loving greed, by M. A. Mendelson.
Review
Bus W p21 Ag 10 '74. R. Schwartz
Tender loving need. Chr Today 18:29 Jl 5
'74
Texas home for Jewish aged has residents'
Bill of rights. il Aging 235:12-13 My '74
Waiting for the end: on nursing homes. B.
Jacoby. il N Y Times Mag p 13-15+ Mr 31
'74
Fires and fire protection
Nixon approves fire safety loans to aid
nursing homes. Aging 233:12 Mr '74
Nursing home association will burn down a
nursing home. il Aging 239:7 S '74
NUT trees
Nut trees of the Northeast. L. H. MacDaniels.
il Conservationist 29:22-4 D '74
See also
Chestnut trees
NUTCRACKER; ballet. See Ballets—Criticisms
NUTRIENT labeling of foods. See Food—La-
beling
NUTRITION
Answers to frequently asked questions on
nutrition. il Good H 179:228 N '74
Beauty: you are what you eat. il Seventeen
33:100-1 Je '74
Buying beef: how much is enough? Con-
sumer Rep 39:666-8 S '74
Food and nutrition. Consumers Res Mag 57:
60-7 O '74
Here's what you should know about vege-
tarianism. D. Grotta-Kurska. il Todays
Health 52:18-21 O '74
National nutrition. C. Holden. Science 183:
1062 Mr 15 '74
Natural things to do. Harp Baz 107:81+ O '74
Notes on nutrition for your family's health
(cont) E. R. Trescher. House & Gard 145:
14+ Mr; 20+ Ap; 16+ My; 146:16+ S; 20+
O; 36+ N '74
Nutrition. R. M. Deutsch. PTA Mag 69:6 S;
9 O; 6 N '74
Nutrition and new food technology. R. R.
Gutierrez and T. C. Byerly. Science 184:
186-8 Ap 12 '74
Nutrition and the brain. J. D. Fernstrom
and R. J. Wurtman. il Sci Am 230:84-91
bibl(p 124) F '74; Summary. BioScience 24:
298 My '74
Nutrition; special issue. il Sr Schol 104:4-
12+ F 28 '74
Nutritional labeling is not a guarantee of
quality! Consumers Res Mag 58:2+ Ja '75
Smart eating; questions and answers (cont
O) Let's talk about food; questions and
answers. P. L. White. See issue of Today's
Health

Labels at left margin:
SUBJECT HEADING
TITLE
AUTHOR
MAGAZINE
VOLUME NUMBER
PAGES
DATE

Who's who in the world of natural health
and beauty. D. Lawson. Harp Baz 107:88+
O '74
See also
Aged—Nutrition
Athletes—Nutrition
Breakfasts
Children—Nutrition
Diet
Food habits
Food values
Infants—Nutrition
Malnutrition
Proteins
Starvation
Vitamins
Woman—Nutrition
NUTRITION and heart disease. See Heart—
Diseases—Nutritional aspects
NUTRITION and intellect. See Intellect—Nu-
tritional aspects
NUTRITION of plants. See Plants—Nutrition
NUTRITION policy
Food and nutrition: is America due for a
national policy? C. Holden. Science 184:
548-50 My 3 '74
Food: fashion and fact; hearings of the
Select committee on nutrition and human
needs. J. Miller. Progressive 38:8-9 Ag '74
For the poor: more hunger. il Time 104:
49 Jl 1 '74
Hunger at home. Commonweal 100:419-20 Ag
9 '74
Hunger: domestic and global links. A. Simon.
Chr Cent 91:759-1 S 25 '74
Let 'em eat Alpo. Nation 219:5 Jl 6 '74
Nutrition dilemma. C. Pierre. Sat R World
1:53-5 My 18 '74
Politics of food: National nutrition policy
study. J. Cross. Nation 219:114-16 Ag 17
'74
See also
United States—Congress—Senate—Nutrition
and human needs. Select committee on
NUTRITION problems
Early protein lack: malevolent effects. il Sci
N 106:229-30 O 12 '74
See also
Underdeveloped areas—Nutrition problems
Africa, Sub-Saharan
Geography of malnutrition in Africa south
of the Sahara. J. M. May. bibl il Focus
25:1-10 S '74
United States
Helping the hungry. M. K. Lally. America
131:253 N 2 '74
Silent crisis. Commonweal 99:523-4 Mr 1 '74
NUTRITION research
Starve the tumor, feed the rat: nutritional
disease control. Sci N 106:91 Ag 10 '74
NUTS
See also
Nut trees
Peanuts
NUTT, James
Art. L. Alloway. Nation 219:317-18 O 5 '74 •
Art. K. Evett. New Repub 172:31-2 Ja 4 '75 •
NUTT, Mary E.
New themes, old techniques. Writer 87:12-14
Je '74
NYBURG, Mary
International dept. new ACC/WCC hookup.
Craft Horiz 34:7 Ap '74
NYE, Joseph Samuel, 1937-
Multinational corporations in world politics.
For Affairs 53:153-75 O '74
NYERGES, Christopher J.
Desert sanctuary of Joshua Tree. il Nat
Parks & Con Mag 48:4-8 N '74
Glacier National Park: a lifetime of memories.
il Nat Parks & Con Mag 48:4-8 Je '74
NYQUIST, Ewald B.
Nontraditional approaches. il Todays Educ
63:63-6 N '74
NYSTRAND, Martin
Lesson plans for the open classroom. il Engl J
63:79-81 My '74

O

O, the big-time game-time show-time roll;
story. See Wolfe, T. K.
OAS. See Organization of American states
OCAW. See Oil, chemical and atomic workers
international union
OCIR'S Manufacturers funny car champion-
ships. See Drag racing
ODC. See Overseas development council
OECD. See Organization for economic coopera-
tion and development

As you develop your list of books and articles for research, make certain that you take down *complete* information on each item. For books, this will include:

author
title
publisher
place of publication
date of publication

For articles, you should have:

author
title of article
name of magazine or newspaper
volume number (if available)
date
page numbers of article

It is useful to put information about each source on a 3 by 5-inch *index card*. Such cards can be bought in most bookstores and stationery stores. Information that you put on an index card might look like this:

By putting the last name of the author first, and underlining it, you will be able to alphabetize entries easily when it comes time to prepare your bibliography.

4. Find your books and articles and take notes.

The best way to take notes is on 5 by 8-inch note cards. In preparing these cards, observe the following guidelines.

a. Have only *one* piece of information on each card.
b. Try to have *subtopics* listed at the top of the card. This will permit you to arrange your cards in groups. It will also help to organize the research paper itself.
c. You can list three types of information on your notecards: direct quotations, summaries (or paraphrases) of material, and your own ideas.
d. Be certain to write the author's name and a page number from your source on each card. (Complete information on the source should already have been put on your index card.)

The sample note card printed below sugests a good arrangement for research information.

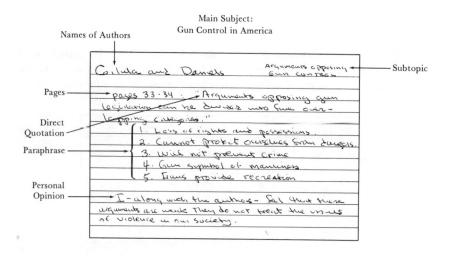

When you have completed all your research, organize your notes under the various subtopics or subheadings that you have established. If necessary, try to combine some subtopics and eliminate others so that you have between three and five major categories for discussion. You are now ready to develop an outline for the research essay.

5. *Prepare an outline.*

The usefulness of an outline in essay writing has already been explained (see pp. 181–183). With the research essay, you need to organize a large bulk of material in a clear way. Therefore, an outline is especially valuable in this instance. If you have used subheadings on your notecards, the preparation of the outline for the research essay should be easy. Simply consult these subheadings, try to determine their best order of arrangement, and then develop an outline using the subheadings as topics for the essay.

6. Write a Rough Draft of the Essay

The trick here is to follow your outline closely and to include your quoted and paraphrased material in the right places. Try to avoid too heavy a reliance on mere quotation and paraphrase. If you rely exclusively on quoted material and fail to acknowledge it, you will be guilty of *plagiarism* (copying material and passing it off as your own). At this point, do not worry about footnoting your material. However, it will help to put an asterisk (*) next to all material that you plan to footnote.

7. Revise the Essay and Add Footnotes.

Revise your essay in keeping with the guidelines for the complete essay given on pages 195–196. Then add your footnote numbers to the essay and prepare a separate page for complete footnote information. (Consult the sample research paper at the end of this section to see how this procedure works.)

Your footnoted information usually will come from four sources: books, magazines, newspapers, and encyclopedias. Here is how a sample footnote looks for each of the sources. Notice that the form for footnoting changes, depending on the type of source consulted.

FOOTNOTING A BOOK

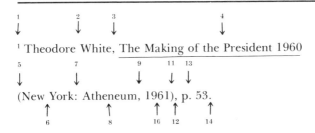

1   number of your footnote; always raise it slightly
2   author: first name followed by last name
3   comma
4   title of book underlined

5   open parenthesis
6   city of publication
7   colon
8   name of publishing company
9   comma
10 date of publication
11 close parenthesis
12 comma
13 period after abbreviation; always abbreviate *page*
14 period at end of page number

FOOTNOTING A MAGAZINE ARTICLE

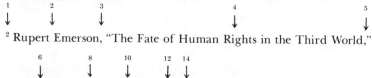

1   number of your footnote
2   author: first name followed by last name
3   comma
4   title of article with quotation marks
5   comma inside quotation marks
6   title of magazine
7   comma
8   volume number
9   open parenthesis
10 month or season of publication
11 comma
12 year of publication
13 close parenthesis
14 comma
15 page number (do not use p. for magazine articles)

Hint: Some magazines (especially the weekly magazines) do not name the writer of the article. In such a case, start the footnote with the title of the article.

FOOTNOTING A NEWSPAPER ARTICLE

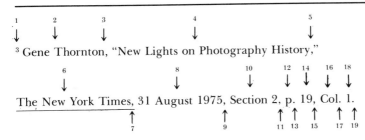

1. footnote number
2. author
3. comma
4. title of article with quotation marks
5. comma inside quotation marks
6. title of newspaper underlined
7. comma
8. date
9. comma
10. part of newspaper
11. comma
12. abbreviation for *page*
13. period
14. page number
15. comma
16. abbreviation for *column*
17. period
18. column number
19. period

Hint: Many newspaper articles are not signed. In such a case, start the footnote with the title of the article.

FOOTNOTING AN ENCYCLOPEDIA ENTRY

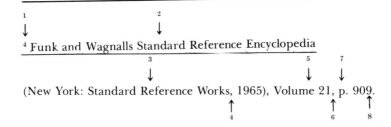

1 footnote number
2 name of encyclopedia
3 publishing information in parentheses
4 comma
5 volume number
6 comma
7 abbreviation for *page*
8 period

Hint: Some encyclopedia contain signed articles. If you encounter an author's name and article title, then these must be listed at the start of your footnote.

Shortening the Second Reference

Once you have given complete footnote information about a book, you can give a shortened footnote if you have to cite that source again. For all additional references to a source, simply give the author and the page number.

First Reference (complete information)	[1] Theodore White, *The Making of the President 1960* (New York: Atheneum, 1961), p. 53.
Second Reference (shortened information)	[2] White, p. 127. However, if you are using several books, or articles by the same author, you must include the title of the work referred to as well as the author's last name. Otherwise the reader will not know which of the author's works you are referring to.

There was a time when writers used the Latin terms *ibid.* ("the same source as listed in the last footnote") and *op. cit.* ("in a work already listed, but not necessarily the last one"). However, these terms are not being used as frequently as they once were.

Guidelines for footnoting

In adding footnotes to your research paper, remember that they are needed for:

1. Direct quotations from sources;
2. A key idea that you have picked up from another writer in the course of your research;
3. Material that you have paraphrased (put into your own words) from other sources.

---

8. *Prepare the Bibliography*

Your bibliography is a list of all works that you have consulted. It comes at the end of your paper. Remember that it frequently contains more material than that listed in your footnotes. Moreover, the form of the bibliography differs from the form used in preparing footnotes.

For entries in bibliographies you must:

1. Arrange all works alphabetically according to an author's last name (or according to the title of a work if there is no author).
2. Indent everything in an entry that comes after the first line.
3. If you are typing, double-space every line and leave double spaces between entries.
4. Punctuate with *periods* after three main divisions in each entry— author, title, and publishing information.

You can see how an entry in a bibliography differs from a footnote:

Footnote	Theodore White, *The Making of the President 1960* (New York:
Form	Atheneum, 1961), p. 53.
Bibliography	White, Theodore. *The Making of the President*
Form	*—1960.* New York: Atheneum, 1961.

period   no parentheses
instead of
comma

The sample research paper in this section has a complete bibliography for you to use as a model.

> *Hint:* Preparing footnotes and entries in a bibliography can be complicated. For an inexpensive guide to *all* forms in footnoting and bibliographic entries, buy *The MLA Style Sheet,* (second edition). This 48-page pamphlet gives information on preparing term papers and can be bought in most college bookstores.

37.2 The Short Research Paper: A Model

This model paper will give you an idea of the techniques that go into the making of a solid research essay.

Football: The Popularization of Violence
Deborah Beuther

"Hit 'em hard!" I shouted, as I stood there with both feet over the sideline. The score was 24–20 in our favor, and the outcome would determine whether or not we had a spot in the playoffs. Now only 22 seconds remained, and the clock was stopped as time was called. The opposing quarterback called the huddle; then the team came out in a wishbone-T offense. Once again, the quarterback called the signals. He then dropped back to pass, was hit as he released the pass, and the ball was intercepted by our cornerback on the 2-yard line. I was overcome; my first impulse was to hit a girl who had previously passed a vulgar remark, saying that we would lose. But she had disappeared into the crowd. Anyway, we had won! It was a long, tiring battle which left several players seriously injured, but it was over.

Although only a spectator at this particular game, I felt very much a part of the team. Perhaps it was all the screaming, jumping, and waiting I had done that made me feel like I, too, was on that playing field. But I am not the only one who subscribes to this type of violence. There are, by far, many others who are just as guilty and partake of such a violent sport. For example, "more than 1,100,000 fans witnessed National Football League games during the 1938 season, or about ten times as many people as attended in 1921, the first season."[1] Today, because of media coverage and the increase in the number of teams, fields, and stadiums, this figure is even greater. Upwards of 70,000,000 people watch the annual Super Bowl Game. This is a significant statistic because most experimental studies suggest that television violence stimulates aggressive behavior.[2] Thus millions are attached to the most violent American sport; and hundreds of thousands of boys and men actually play the game.

Football, which in one form or another has been played in America since 1609,[3] is assuredly a game involving violence. As one expert puts it, "Football is a game of contact and one is either doing the hitting or is getting hit."[4] The team that hits hardest is usually the winner. The men who play are literally on the battlefield. They are well conditioned, strong, and aggressive. Each one is a warrior hero in his own right, with a position similar to those of infantry in warfare. They do hard, brutal, bitter fighting for victory. But is their struggle for success a real victory?

Football players, like army recruits, are mentally and physically conditioned to be aggressive. To be a great warrior hero, one must be vicious and overpowering in his actions. As Bob Lilly admits, "It's reached the point now where you've got to be half mean. You have to feel that every time you get a chance to take a shot at somebody you have to take it."[5] Bob Brown illuminates the issue even more graphically: "I like to compare my style to a sledgehammer. It's not fancy, it's crude-looking, but it works."[6]

The use of violent force upon his opponent is important to the success of the football warrior, but equally important is his ability to protect himself. "American football is without any question the leader among all team sports as a cause of injury."[7] Despite the elaborate equipment used, increases in injuries continue each year. Regardless of his armament, the warrior is vulnerable; the wounded who observe the action from the sidelines of the weekly battlefield increase as the football season advances.

Players and spectators alike have a complicity in this savage sport. At the same time, all have a choice as to whether or not they want to partake in this violence, as in the case of murder. But perhaps we have a need for "controlled" violence, either as participants or as empathetic fans. Perhaps we will continue to populate the sidelines, shouting in unison, "Hit 'em hard!"

Footnotes

[1] Robert B. Weaver, *Amusements and Sports in American Life* (Westport, Conn.: Greenwood Press, 1968), p. 124.

[2] "TV Violence: Appalling," *U.S. News and World Report* (October 6, 1969), 55–56.

[3] Ibid., p. 112.

[4] Gomer Jones, Offensive and Defensive Line Play Englewood Cliffs, N.J.: Prentice Hall, 1961), p. 10.

[5] Barry Stainback, *How the Pros Play Football* (New York: Random House, 1970), p. 10.

[6] Ibid. pp. 94–95

[7] Allan J. Ryan, *Medical Care of the Athlete* (New York, 1962), p. 272.

Bibliography

Gerhart, Douglas. *Coaching an Explosive Passing Offense.* Englewood Cliffs, N.J.: Prentice Hall, 1969.

Jones, Gomer. *Offensive and Defensive Line Play.* Englewood Cliffs, N.J.: Prentice Hall, 1961.

Ryan, Allan J., *Medical Care of the Athelete.* New York, 1962.

Stainback, Barry. *How the Pros Play Football.* New York: Random House, 1970.

"TV Violence: Appalling," *U.S. News and World Report,* October 6, 1969, 55–56.

Weaver, Robert B. *Amusements and Sports in American Life.* Westport, Conn.: Greenwood Press, 1968.

Application 1 Answer the following questions.

a. In what ways is the short research paper like an ordinary essay? In what ways does it differ? _____

_____

b. In terms of the way this research essay is organized, what patterns are used by the writer?_____

_____

c. Is the comparison that the writer uses in this paper an effective one?_____

_____

d. What are the similarities and differences between the footnotes and the bibliography? Is there an entry that is incomplete? _____

_____

e. Why does the writer begin and end this paper on a personal note, and with the statement, "Hit 'em hard!"? _____

_____

Writing Project   Take any subject that is of special interest to you and write a short 500 to 750 word research paper on it. Use at least five footnotes in the paper and have a minimum of five entries in your bibliography.

CHAPTER 38

Writing About Literature

Most college students take introduction to literature courses. Many take more specialized courses in fiction, poetry, or drama; or they take survey courses of American literature, British literature, or modern literature. In all these courses you must know how to analyze literary works. The section in this *Handbook* that deals with simple analysis (see pp. 173–174) explains that ordinary analysis involves the how and why of things. Literary analysis also deals with an important "what"—what is the meaning of a particular work? In literary analysis you deal both with the meaning of a work and how the writer presents it. The following guidelines will prepare you for literary analysis.

38.1. Guide to Good Literary Analysis

1. Briefly explain *what* the main meaning of the work is. (The main meaning of a literary work is called its *theme*.)
2. Show *how* the writer arrives at the meaning through a variety of technical devices. In order to handle this aspect of analysis properly, you will need to master the list of literary terms on pp. 215–218.
3. Explain *why* the work you are analyzing is successful or unsuccessful, important or unimportant. In other words, you have to do more than explain meanings and processes. You have to render a verdict on the relative importance and originality of the work. Here there is room for personal opinion (subjectivity) as well as for a detached view (objectivity).
4. Be sure to mention anything special about the author's life and times that helps to explain his or her work.
5. Avoid at all costs a mere summary of the work. Don't just tell what happens in a story, play, or poem. This is *not* analysis. It is just a retelling of events. If you are going to summarize something for the benefit of a reader who is not familiar with the work, then do it briefly.

38.2. A Sample Literary Analysis

The short sketch below was written by Ernest Hemingway and appeared originally in a collection of the author's stories, *In Our Time*. Read the sketch and then look at the analysis of it. Answer the questions that follow the analysis.

They shot the six cabinet ministers at half-past six in the morning against the wall of a hospital. There were pools of water in the courtyard. There were wet dead leaves on the paving of the courtyard. It rained hard. All the shutters of the hospital were nailed shut. One of the ministers was sick with typhoid. Two soldiers carried him downstairs and out into the rain. They tried to hold him up against the wall but he sat down in a puddle of water. The other five stood very quietly against the wall. Finally the officer told the soldiers it was no good trying to make him stand up. When they fired the first volley he was sitting down in the water with his head on his knees.

ANALYSIS

Ernest Hemingway's brief account of six cabinet ministers who are killed by a firing squad suggests that death in the modern world can be sick, ugly, and degrading. The tone of this story is highly pessimistic, and this tone reinforces the dull, depressing mood of the tale. The atmosphere, filled with images like "wet dead leaves," creates an almost hopeless sense of things. It prepares the reader for the death of the ministers. Hemingway adds a note of irony to their deaths by mentioning that they were lined up against the wall of a hospital. As he says, "All the shutters were nailed shut." A hospital is supposed to help people, but in this instance it is worthless for the victims of violence. The sick cabinet minister, who stands out from the rest of the characters, becomes the symbol of all individuals who are killed without dignity in this world. In fact, his sickness might reflect the larger sickness of our times. Hemingway, in an extremely short amount of space, and in language that is simple, direct and forceful, seems to be telling us that we all run the risk of dying like animals. The sketch is a brilliant presentation of violence and death. As such, it seems to reflect personal preoccupations that ultimately led to Hemingway's own violent end.

Application Write out answers to the questions that appear below.

a. Does the writer like Hemingway's story? How can you tell? _____

_____

_____

b. Is there any summary in this analysis? If so, where? _____

_____

_____

c. According to the writer, what is the *theme* of Hemingway's story?

_____

_____

d. Why does the writer quote from Hemingway's sketch? Why is this an effective device? _____

_____

e. Does the writer provide us with any special information about Hemingway? _____

_____

f. How does the writer reveal a knowledge of the technical devices that Hemingway uses? List some technical words that seem important in the analysis of literature. _____

_____

_____

_____

_____

38.3. Literary Terms

Every subject—whether it is literature, psychology, or physics—has its own vocabulary. The purpose of this vocabulary is to label and explain information special to a particular field. For instance, "supply and demand" is a term from economics. "Schizophrenia" is a term that is used in psychology. In literature, there are many special terms that are used in analysis. Twenty of the most common literary terms are listed below; try to form the habit of using them when you write literary analyses of stories, poems, plays, or films.

Characterization

Characterization is the way in which the writer creates believable people. Critics frequently speak of "round" and "flat" characters. A round character is a fully developed personality; a flat character tends to be more of a type. In a play or a story, we don't know as much about flat characters as we do about round ones.

Comedy

This is one of the two major categories of literature (*tragedy* is the other). A literary work that is comic tends to involve us in humor and laughter. Comedy can also be used to reveal the weaknesses of individuals and classes of people. The endings in comic works are often happy or corrective.

Conflict

Fiction and drama cannot exist without conflict. Conflict involves a clash of things. Typical forms of conflict in literature are men and women versus society; man versus woman; men and women versus nature; men and women versus ideas; man or woman versus self.

Dialogue

Dialogue is the language which characters actually speak. It is set off from the rest of the literary work by quotation marks. Dialogue tells us a great deal about the personalities of the characters and about their motivations, and ultimately about the conflicts in the literary work under analysis.

Foreshadowing

This device is commonly employed to give the reader hints about the climax or the final outcome of the literary work. Foreshadowing makes us anticipate the ending in a literary work.

Genre

Genre is a French word which means "type" or "form." It is said that there are three major genres in literature—fiction, poetry, and drama. However, such literary works as essays, autobiography, and editorial writing could also qualify as genres. We expect different things from different literary forms, and it is always good to keep this in mind when writing literary analyses.

Imagery

Imagery is vivid description. It is making a picture with words. Imagery tends to appeal to our senses—sight, sound, touch, taste, and smell.

Irony

When we say that a situation is "ironic," we mean that the intended meaning is the direct opposite of what is normally expected. Thus

Hemingway used irony in his sketch by having the cabinet ministers shot against the wall of a hospital. In literary analysis, there are many forms of irony: for example, we speak of *irony of situation* (like that in Hemingway's tale), *verbal irony* (as when a character tells a stupid person that he is clever), and *irony of fate* (when a character's destiny is the opposite of what he or she expected).

Metaphor

A metaphor is a form of figurative language that makes a comparison, as in "She is a fox." In other words, the woman is compared to a fox.

Mood

The mood is the "atmosphere" created in a literary work.

Motif

A recurring pattern that the writer employs through the work is a motif. In Hemingway's sketch, we might say that "wetness" constitutes a motif. Consequently, a motif tends to underscore the main theme.

Narrative

A narrative is the story or events in a literary work.

Plot

The plot is the way that the story or play is structured or put together. We often say that literary plots have a beginning, a middle, and an end. But sometimes plots start in the middle of things. Sometimes they start at the end of things and then through *flashbacks* (the telling of earlier episodes) complete the narration.

Point of view

In fiction, the angle from which the story is told is the point of view. Sometimes the story is told by the "I" narrator; this is called the first-person point of view. At other times the story is told from the "he, she, it, they" point of view; this is called the third-person point of view. Both methods have advantages and disadvantages.

Simile

A simile is a form of comparison that uses the words *like* or *as* to make the connection. If we were to say, "She is *like* a fox," we would be turning our earlier metaphor into a simile.

Stanza

A stanza is a group of lines in a poem. Such units are separated from other units (or stanzas) by spaces on the page.

Symbol

A symbol is an object used to represent something that is abstract. For instance, the cross is a symbol of Christianity.

Theme

This is the main idea in a literary work. The theme is what the writer is saying about his subject.

Tone

The writer's attitude toward his material is his tone. A writer's tone might be critical, sarcastic, approving, despairing, or any number of things.

Tragedy

A tragedy is a serious literary work that has a disastrous or unhappy conclusion.

Application Write a short analysis of the following poem. Make a deliberate effort to use at least five of the literary terms listed above.

Proletarian Portrait

A big young bareheaded woman
in an apron

Her hair slicked back standing
on the street

One stockinged foot toeing
the sidewalk

Her shoe in her hand. Looking
intently into it

She pulls out the paper insole
to find the nail

That has been hurting her

William Carlos Williams

_____

_____

_____

_____

_____

_____

_____

_____

_____

_____

_____

CHAPTER 39

Writing for the Social Sciences

The social sciences consist of the following fields: anthropology, sociology, psychology, economics, and political science. In addition, history is considered by some to be a social science. All areas in social science are linked in that they study men and women, their behavior and their problems. Social science explores the nature of our society, and the ways in which individuals are shaped by social, political, economic, and cultural forces.

When you write for any social science course, it is best to be somewhat "scientific." This is because the social sciences attempt to be as systematic as possible in the way that they explore problems. Although it is sometimes useful to relate your findings in personal terms, not all teachers will accept such subjective interpretations of material.

In social science writing, you should apply the art of analysis that has been mentioned in previous sections of the *Handbook*. You should learn how *to observe, to survey material,* to *work with statistics*. Finally, you should learn the principles of sound logic. Such skills—along with your mastery of social science vocabulary—will make you an effective writer in social science courses.

What Is the Scientific Method?

There has always been discussion about whether the social sciences are "true sciences." Nevertheless, the social sciences do utilize the scientific method, and consequently it is worthwhile to know some basic principles that you should follow in attempting to make your social science papers clear and solid. Material in such papers, if handled properly, will conform to the basic outlines of the scientific method. What this means is that your writing will be systematic and exact. Of course, on a broader level, a social science paper reflects generally the methods that go into all good writing.

Here are some hints for applying the scientific method to the social sciences:

1. Scientific information aims at description, explanation, and prediction. Here, forms of analysis (especially cause and effect analysis) are very valuable.

2. Try to be objective in your presentation of material. Remember that what you present in a social science paper should enable any reader (with the proper background) to observe and test it as well, and obtain similar results. Therefore, avoid mere impressions and weak generalizations when writing for the social sciences.

3. Be certain to give enough data in a social science paper to prove your main ideas and make the reader feel that your information is reliable. In other words, the proper use of examples (see pp. 162–163) is important in social science papers. Moreover, the more you can learn about the techniques of experimentation and statistics, the better your social science paper will be.

4. One of the most important characteristics of the scientific method is the systemic presentation of knowledge. A well-structured account of facts in a social science paper is therefore required. Facts must be arranged and properly classified.

5. Explanations in social science papers must take place through a process of *deduction*. This involves the writer in a movement from the general to the specific. The writer must take a known law or theory and then proceed to obtain observable facts that permit a logical outcome.

The above outline of elements in the scientific method can serve as a guide, but remember that you cannot be absolutely scientific in the social sciences. Because each individual is unique in a social structure, this fact should be taken into account whenever you are dealing with concepts in the social sciences.

Application   The selection below attempts to analyze how violence on television effects children. Read the paragraph and then answer the questions that follow it.

In a famous experiment, researchers at the Stanford University psychological laboratories proved that children are more aggressive when they watch televised violence than when they do not. Four groups of children were placed in test rooms. Three groups were exposed to real and televised violence in which an adult kicked and punched a large Bobo doll. The fourth group—the control group—was not exposed to any form of violence. Next, each child was taken to an observation room, where he was watched by psychologists who recorded his behavior. In this observation room there were both "peaceful" toys (crayons, cars, tea sets) and "violent" toys (hammers, guns, and similar items). Each child spent twenty minutes in the observation room. During this time, the children who watched the attack on the Bobo doll demonstrated twice as much aggressiveness as those in the control groups. The results of this test forced the researchers to conclude that there is indeed a connection between violence on television and aggressiveness in children.

a. Of the five areas of social science mentioned in the introduction to this section, which ones relate to the paragraph? _____

b. Does the writer attempt to be "scientific" in the presentation of material? How do you know? _____

_____

_____

c. What is a "control group?" _____

_____

d. Does the writer provide enough data in this paragraph, or would you want more information? _____

_____

e. Are you satisfied with the conclusion reached in the last sentence?

_____

_____

Using Statistics

Statistics are facts and numbers that have been assembled and classified in order to provide important information about a given subject. Although statistics can be useful in any form of writing, they are especially valuable in social science writing. They add an element of objectivity to any social science problem that you are investigating.

In order to use statistics effectively you must:

1. Learn how to read statistical tables and graphs.
2. Present statistical information clearly in your own writing.
3. Avoid the temptation to merely "pile up" numbers and figures.
4. Always interpret the statistical information.
5. Use reliable sources, which you should mention in the course of your writing.

Application 1 Here is a chart which reveals the attitudes of Americans on major issues of national concern.

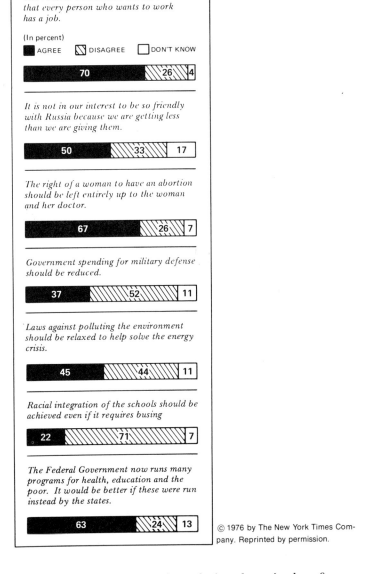

The Federal Government should see to it that every person who wants to work has a job.

(In percent)
■ AGREE ▧ DISAGREE ☐ DON'T KNOW

70 | 26 | 4

It is not in our interest to be so friendly with Russia because we are getting less than we are giving them.

50 | 33 | 17

The right of a woman to have an abortion should be left entirely up to the woman and her doctor.

67 | 26 | 7

Government spending for military defense should be reduced.

37 | 52 | 11

Laws against polluting the environment should be relaxed to help solve the energy crisis.

45 | 44 | 11

Racial integration of the schools should be achieved even if it requires busing

22 | 71 | 7

The Federal Government now runs many programs for health, education and the poor. It would be better if these were run instead by the states.

63 | 24 | 13

On the basis of this chart, write a paragraph analyzing the attitudes of Americans on key issues. Make use of statistics in your paper.

_____

_____

_____

_____

_____

_____

_____

_____

_____

_____

Application 2   Write definitions for the following social science terms. These words can be found in your dictionary if you need help.

1. adaptation   _____

2. anarchism   _____

3. anthropology   _____

4. capitalism   _____

5. class   _____

6. communism   _____

7. culture   _____

8. democracy   _____

9. dictatorship   _____

10. economics _____

_____

11. elite _____

_____

12. environment _____

_____

13. evolution _____

_____

14. motivation _____

_____

15. nationalism _____

_____

16. oligarchy _____

_____

17. perception _____

_____

18. personality _____

_____

19. political science _____

_____

20. psychology _____

_____

21. race _____

_____

22. racism _____

_____

23. role _____

_____

24. sex _____

_____

25. socialism

_____

_____

26. socialization

_____

_____

27. status

_____

_____

28. stereotype

_____

_____

29. supply and demand

_____

_____

30. values

_____

_____

CHAPTER 40

Writing for the Sciences

In college science courses, in technical and engineering subjects, and in many related job situations, you may have to do some technical writing. Good technical writing reflects many of the qualities of sound writing already discussed in this *Handbook*. However, certain qualities of sound technical writing should be emphasized:

1. *Good technical writing is concrete and precise.* It employs words carefully to describe or explain exactly what has been observed or discovered.
2. *Good technical writing is direct.* It comes to the point quickly and doesn't waste words.
3. *Good technical writing is impersonal.* It avoids the use of the first person ("I"). The preference is scientific writing is for the elimination of all personal references.
4. *Good technical writing is based on facts.* It is based on truths drawn from observation, experimentation, and the proven research of others.
5. *Good technical writing is logical.* Conclusions derive from evidence that has been presented systematically.

Sound technical writing also reflects the scientific method (see pp. 220–221). The scientific method in technical writing involves a series of steps: (1) the statement of the problem; (2) the background of the problem; (3) procedure; (4) observations; (5) conclusions; and (6) discussion. This progression will be reflected in the analysis of the laboratory report that appears in this section.

In scientific writing, you do not want to be fancy. The best style is a simple style. Frequently you have a complicated subject to deal with, and the best way for you to make it understood by the reader is to explain it in clear language. You can be just as effective with a simple style of writing as with a more colorful one. Technical writing does not call for poetic comparisons or special emotional effects. It does call for simplicity and clarity in the presentation of materials.

40.1. The Laboratory Report

The laboratory report is the most prevalent form of technical writing in college. It presents information on experiments that you conduct in such science courses as chemistry, physics, botany, and zoology. A typical format for the laboratory report appears below.

Title—Here state the name of the experiment.

Purpose—Express briefly the objective(s) of the experiment.

Procedure—Cite where the procedure can be found, as well as any modifications you may have made in the printed procedure. If only parts of the procedure were carried out, that should be indicated here also.

Data—This may include observations made during the course of the experiment; numerical data collected, such as weights and volumes; charts or graphs constructed in the course of the experiment; and any other relevant materials.

Calculations—When an experiment involves calculations, they need to be shown here. Actual computation need not be shown, but the mathematical set-up should be shown. Sometimes it is helpful to the instructor to see the computation, since errors frequently can be detected here.

Conclusions—This section is reserved for conclusions reached in the lab. The conclusions should relate in some obvious manner to the purpose of the experiment. Sometimes conclusions may include answers to questions included in the experimental procedure.

Discussion—This may include your own evaluation of the experiment, explanation of sources of error or of poor results, answers to questions about the experiment, and other items as the instructor may direct.

In some instances, not all categories will be applicable to the experiment being conducted. However, in every lab report, you should present the title, purpose, procedure, data, and conclusions.

The following is a sample lab report written by a student. The results reported by the student are not necessarily the results to be expected if *you* were to carry out this experiment. They are merely for illustrative purposes.

Lab. Report #1.

Title: Identification of a Substance

Purpose: To identify an unknown substance on the basis of certain physical properties.

Procedure: Lab. Manual by Hend & Nebergall, Exp. 3, p. 14-19, Parts 1, 2B, 4 and 5.

Data:

Substance	Solubility in		
	Water	Benzene	alcohol
Naphthalene	insol	sol	insol
Paraffin Oil	insol	sol	insol
Unknown #35	sol	sol	insol

Density of Unknown #35 (a liquid)

weight of empty beaker	75.38 g
weight of beaker & unknown	83.12 g
weight of unknown	7.74 g
Volume of unknown	10.0 ml
Density of unknown	0.774 g/ml

Calculation: $83.12\,g$
$-75.38\,g$
$7.74\,g$ = weight of unknown

Density = $\dfrac{Mass}{Volume}$ = $\dfrac{7.74\,g}{10.0\,ml}$ = $0.774\ g/ml$

Conclusion: Unknown #25 is methyl alcohol because experimental results agree best with data given for methyl alcohol:

	Density	Boiling Pt.	Solubility
Unknown #25	0.774		
Methyl Alcohol	0.79	64°C	s s s
		65°C	s s s

Discussion: When the liquid began to boil the temperature was still rising rapidly and it was hard to determine at exactly what temperature the liquid boiled freely. Condensation on the thermometer also made reading it difficult.

40.2. Technical Essays and Reports

Unlike lab reports, which tend to be "shorthand" presentations of the results of an experiment conducted in the laboratory, technical essays and reports are standard compositions. They include the results of laboratory experimentation and other forms of research as well. This additional research material might include:

1. Facts from publications like scientific magazines and journals.
2. Results of questionnaires and interviews.
3. Charts, tables, and diagrams presenting statistics.
4. Recommendations (especially for applied research projects designed for practical purposes).
5. Bibliographic references to and summaries of material located in scientific indexes and abstracts. There are many such reference books, among them: *Biological and Agricultural Index, Bibliography of Scientific and Technical Reports, Chemical Abstracts, Engineering Index, The Industrial Arts Index,* and *U.S. Government Research Reports.*

Technical essays and reports can present the results of an experiment or research program, solve a problem, evaluate a product, recommend the development of a product, and review research. They can take the form of in-house *memoranda* (see p. 243), scientific reports divided into major sections, or papers written for scientific or technical journals. If you have to write a technical report or an essay for an instructor, make certain that you know the form that the report should be presented in.

A typical technical report will reflect the following divisions, although other orders are possible:

a. Title page.
b. Table of Contents (divided into categories).
c. Abstract. (This is a very brief summary of the main items in the report. It permits the reader, whether a college professor or a company executive, to size up important data on a single page.)
d. Introduction, describing the hypothesis or scientific problem to be tested or investigated.
e. Report, stressing methods and procedures.
f. Findings.
g. Interpretations and recommendations.
h. Appendixes (consisting of charts, tables, graphs, and support material).

It is important to have categories or subtitles (which are like chapter headings) in your table of contents.

CONTENTS

ILLUSTRATIONS

In this sense, the contents page of a technical report differs from that of the ordinary research or college term paper, which should *not* be divided into categories. The technical report has a fairly rigid format; always know what is required of you in this area.

Application 1 Examine one of the scientific reference books listed on page 231 or below and make a report to the class on its contents.

Aerospace Engineering Review
Applied Mechanics Reviews
Applied Science and Technology Index
Biological Abstracts
Forestry Abstracts
Nuclear Science Abstracts

Application 2 Read an article in a well-known scientific magazine like *Popular Mechanics* or *Scientific American* and then write a short abstract of it.

_____

_____

_____

_____

_____

_____

_____

Application 3   Write a technical report on any research project that you have completed—in the laboratory, at home, or on the job. If you are not scientifically inclined, write about a moderately technical topic like (a) ways to improve gas mileage; (b) preventing damage to lawns; (c) increasing efficiency at work; or (d) the relative merits of suntan lotions (or any other group of products).

CHAPTER 41

Writing
for Business

Many forms of writing help you to succeed in the business world. Some types of writing—for instance, letters of application and résumés—help you to *get* a job. Other types—letters of inquiry, letters of complaint, memos, and order letters—will help you to *keep* the job once you have it; some of these letter forms also enable you to obtain information and make complaints. Therefore, this last section in the *Handbook* is probably the most practical. Only the most common forms of business writing can be treated here. But these forms in themsleves will prove that good writing carries with it benefits for all.

41.1. Selling Yourself: The Letter of Application

Make no mistake about it: when you are applying for a job by letter, you are in the process of selling yourself. Remember that employers are busy; they do not want long letters of application. Therefore, keep your letter of application to one page. In addition, make certain that you present an attractive image of yourself and that you set up the letter correctly. There are essentially two types of letters of application— solicited (written in answer to an advertisement) and unsolicited (written on your own initiative).

If you examine this letter of application, you will be able to determine the guidelines for its proper preparation. Here are some suggestions:

1. Always type *any* business letter.

The Solicited Letter

111-07 66th Avenue
Flushing, N.Y. 11375
January 27, 1977

S 1234 (Times)
New York, N.Y. 10036

Gentlemen:

I read your advertisement in yesterday's *Times* with great interest. As you will see in my résumé, I am majoring in data processing at LaGuardia Community College, from which I will graduate in June, 1975. I've completed with consistently high grades the following programming courses: Cobol, RPG, BAL, and Assembly language.

My work as a lead computer operator for the past six years has allowed me to apply the skills learned in school to the world of business. So far, I've successfully written for my personal use and satisfaction ten programs in Cobol language, which I will gladly bring to show you at your request.

My strong background in operations and the extensive knowledge I acquired in school will, I believe, highly qualify me for the position of programming trainee in your organization.

May I have the opportunity of seeing you in person so that I may discuss this application with you in detail. My telephone number is (212) 896-5125.

Very truly yours,

Peter Dominijanni

---

2. Learn the proper forms for a business letter. In this letter, the form (which is called "semiblock" can be diagramed in the following manner:

return address
date

inside address

salutation (always followed by a
colon)

body of letter (with each paragraph indented)

complimentary close
(ending in comma)

signature

> *Hint:* Other business letter forms include:
>
> a. *block layout*—this differs from semiblock in that the paragraphs in the body of the letter are started flush against the left margin. There is no indentation.
>
> b. *full block:* this layout places *all* information—including the return address and complimentary close—against the left margin.

3. Have an introduction that refers specifically to the advertisement.
4. Be sure to state both your educational and job experience in the body of the letter.
5. Close by asking for an interview and by providing your telephone number.

Application   Select a job advertisement from a local paper and write an imaginary (or real) letter of application for the position. Observe the guidelines previously listed.

The Unsolicited Letter

Although it might seem silly to apply for positions that have not been advertised, an unsolicited letter might just turn up the job you have been looking for. Sometimes vacancies become available at the last minute when someone has been fired or has retired because of illness. Sometimes a prospective employer will take a liking to your letter of application. In any case, your letter will be kept on file in the event that a job does materialize.

Application   Think of a company that you would like to work for and write them a letter of application for a job that would interest you.

41.2. Selling Yourself: The Résumé

A résumé is a summary of your background and work experience. As with the letter of application, the résumé is a form of sales writing: you are trying to sell yourself to a possible employer. As such, the résumé is one of the most important aspects of job hunting and one of the most important things you will write. You should always include a résumé with your letter of application.

SAMPLE RÉSUMÉ

Thomas G. Gillis
15–18 145th Place
Whitestone, NY 11357
Telephone: (212) 672-9639

OBJECTIVE: Accounting Clerk

EDUCATION: LaGuardia Community College; expect to graduate in 1975 with an Associate of Applied Science in Accounting.

Holy Cross High School; graduated in 1969 with an academic diploma.

MAJOR COURSES:
Business Writing
Economics
Accounting Law
Business Management

EXPERIENCE:
Summer, 1973 Merrill, Lynch, Pierce, Fenner & Smith, Inc.,
1 Liberty Plaza, New York. Worked in the Accounting Department. Checked audits and tax returns.

Summer, 1972 *Gimbel's Department Store,*
Broadway and 33rd Street, New York. Worked with the Assistant Sales Manager as a representative of customer complaints.

COLLEGE ACTIVITIES:
President, Accounting Club
Vice-President, Society for the Advancement of Management
Intramural Sports
Chess Club

HOBBIES AND INTERESTS:
Chess, mechanics, business periodicals.

REFERENCES: Mr. Ronald Miller, Chairman of Accounting Department
LaGuardia Community College
35–10 Thomson Avenue
Long Island City, NY 11240

Mr. George Lewis, Teller
First National City Bank
20–44 121st Street
College Point, NY 11356
(212) 746-5329

Mr. Bernard Rieter, Manager
Rieter Quality Foods
14–39 127th Street
College Point, NY 11356
(212) 359-5416

Guide to Writing a Résumé

1. Keep it short—no more than one page. Employers look at *thousands* of résumés. Therefore, in a limited amount of you must make your résumé look distinctive.
2. Include only the most important information (see the sample résumé for guidelines). Contrary to information provided in many business texts, an employer is not interested (yet) in your height, weight, and Social Security number.
3. Always type your résumé, or have it professionally typed and duplicated
4. Make certain the layout is attractive. The spatial effect should be balanced, harmonious, and uncluttered.
5. Emphasize your strong points. (This can be done listing major courses, detailing your work experience, listing significant college activities, and providing references.)

Application   Write a résumé of your own similar to the one in this section.

41.3. Letters of Inquiry

A letter of inquiry is designed to obtain the information you need. In such a letter, you must state your needs clearly so that the receiver knows what you want. Letters of inquiry can be used for both personal and business reasons. When you write such letters, remember to follow the guidelines on form set down on page 235. Moreover, try to have at least three paragraphs in the letter:

Paragraph 1: State courteously the reasons for writing.
Paragraph 2: Clearly state the information or materials that you need. Be as specific as possible in making your request.
Paragraph 3: Express your appreciation in the conclusion. If necessary, indicate that you need the information within a specific period of time.

Here is a sample letter of inquiry, written in block form.

71-11 Yellowstone Boulevard
Forest Hills, New York 11375
February 21, 1975

Mr. John R. Graves
Dean of Admissions
Washington University
34 Lincoln Place
Washington, D.C. 22314

Dear Mr. Graves:

I am entering my third semester at La Guardia Community College as a major in Business Administration and have completed most of the required courses for an A.S. degree.

Your school has been recommended by our guidance department as one of the best business schools in the Washington area. I would like, therefore, to see a copy of your catalogue in order to determine what electives would be most helpful to me if I were to transfer to your school.

Since registration for the spring quarter is scheduled within the next three weeks, I would appreciate receiving a copy of your catalogue as soon as possible.

Thank you in advance for your assistance.

Sincerely,

Patricia M. Quinn

Responding to the Letter of Inquiry

If you receive a letter of inquiry, then you have to answer it clearly. Remember to provide all the information requested, as well as any additional material that has been asked for. If you are unable to provide information, then try to explain why it is not available at the present time.

Here is a reply to the letter of inquiry that was given as a model.

Washington University
34 Lincoln Place
Washington, D.C. 22314
February 26, 1977

Ms. Patricia M. Quinn
71-11 Yellowstone Boulevard
Forest Hills, New York 11375

Dear Ms. Quinn:

Thank you for your letter of February 21 requesting a copy of our catalogue. I presume from your letter that you won't be graduating until June '76, and our catalogue for that time is not ready.

I will, however, send a copy of our current catalogue which does explain in detail what our requirements are for a Bachelor's degree in Business Administration. This catalogue, of course, is subject to change, but I suggest nevertheless that you select your remaining electives so that they meet Washington University's basic requirements for a B.A. in Business Administration. In the meantime, your name has been put on file to receive the '76 catalogue when it is printed.

Thank you, again, for your interest in our school.

Sincerely,

John R. Graves
Dean of Admissions

JRG:ab
Enc.

Application   Pretend that you are planning a short vacation to another part of the state. Write to the State Department of Tourism for vacation ideas and road hints. After you have written this letter, shift roles, and write a response to the letter in which you provide all necessary information. Use the two letters that have been reproduced in this section as models.

41.4. Letters of Complaint

Quite frequently we are dissatisfied with goods or services received. Letters are often needed to solve problems involving damaged goods or items not yet received, especially after telephone calls have failed to produce the desired results. In a letter of complaint, you have to provide correct information. In writing a letter of complaint, try to strike the right tone. You don't want to be too angry, or sarcastic, or threatening, or obscene. You *do* want to be firm and reasonable; moreover, it is always good to have an ace in the hole, as the following letter of complaint reveals.

71-11 Yellowstone Boulevard
Forest Hills, New York 11375
February 21, 1977

Mr. Joseph R. Traub
Furniture Adjustment Manager
Bloomingdale's
1000 Third Avenue
New York, New York 10022

Dear Mr. Traub:

On January 15, I came to your store and spoke with Miss Helen Jones of your furniture adjustment department. My purpose in contacting her was to schedule an appointment for your carpenters to repair damage on my Henredon Canterbury Bedroom Set (Invoice #002378416), which occurred during delivery on the previous day. In so doing, as you can see, I acted within the guidelines of your contract.

It is now 1½ months later and I am asking myself why the appointment of Saturday, February 1 was not kept and whether you plan to schedule another appointment. Oversights are to be expected, of course, considering the great volume of business that you do, but a simple courteous call would have settled the whole matter. (Wouldn't you agree?)

Incidentally, I have received a bill for the furniture for $3,800, but I am holding up payment until it has been repaired. Please contact me at once by calling (212) 723-2019 between 9 A.M. and 5 P.M.

Sincerely,

Patricia M. Quinn

Application   Imagine yourself in Mr. Traub's place. Write a reply to Ms. Quinn's letter of complaint and promise her an immediate adjustment. Assume responsibility for the oversight. Thank Ms. Quinn for her "courtesy." Also assure her that the bill won't become effective until after the repair work has been completed.

41.5. Letters of Collection

Unlike Mr. Traub, whose company was guilty of an oversight in making a repair, you frequently might have to write a letter of collection for money that is owed. Once again, you have to consider your tone and be careful that it is not insulting or bullying. These tactics rarely work with people who owe money. Instead, try to be firm but reasonable, and to persuade the customer that it is in his or her best interest to honor all payments due. The next sample letter achieves this correct tone.

BANKAMERICARD CENTER
P.O. Box 590
Radio City Station
New York, New York 10019
Telephone: (212) 541-7500

May 22, 1977

Mrs. Marie Satriano
63-76 Elwell Crescent
Forest Hills, New York 11375

Re: Account no. 4520-007911

Dear Mrs. Satriano:

We have written reminding you of your outstanding account balance of $125 on two previous occasions.

We regret the necessity of sending this third and final notice, particularly since our records show that you have always been prompt in your payments to us.

We value the goodwill of our customers and if there are any extenuating circumstances, we would gladly make arrangements with you to extend your credit for a period of ninety (90) days.

We are sure you will not want us to go to law and impair your excellent credit rating. We are, therefore, holding your account in abeyance until May 30. If you would like to speak to me about this matter, please call me anytime during office hours at the above number, extension 223.

Yours very truly,

(Mrs.) Carleen Greco
Credit Manager

CG:md

Application Using the preceding letter as a model, write a letter of collection in which you request payment on a bill that is overdue.

41.6. The Memorandum

The memorandum (or memo) is a message that circulates within a business or institution. It is important to describe who it is coming from, to whom it is going, the date it is released, the subject, and the message itself. Many businesses have their own memorandum forms. One such form is reproduced below.

When forms are not available, type the memorandum in the following manner:

To: _____   *Date:* _____

From: _____   *Subject:* _____

(Body)

Application Write a memo to your teacher in which you describe what you plan to write about for a particular assignment.

TO	Harper & Row Publishers	FROM	Fairfield Graphics
	10 East 53rd Street		North Miller Street
	New York, New York 10022		Fairfield, Pa. 17320
	Att: Mr. Kewal Sharma		

SUBJECT _____ ECONOMICS: A READER _____

Message

Please advise the date copy will be received, so that a firm schedule can be issued.

DATE   6/15/77   SIGNED *Roger Wusson*

Reply

DATE   SIGNED

87-RM2   **RETURN THIS COPY TO SENDER**

Terms used in business writing

adjustment letter: written in reply to a letter complaint or to a letter of request; it may grant a request, decline it, or request further information.

application letter: a letter enclosed with a résumé as part of a written job application, it should be included whether the application answers an ad or not and should complement, not duplicate, the résumé.

autobiographical sketch (or "self-evaluation essay"): often requested with academic applications and occasionally job applications; such a sketch is also very useful in sorting out one's assets to prepare the résumé and job application letter, or to prepare for a job interview.

blocked paragraphs: increasingly standard format in business correspondence; each paragraph begins at the left margin without indentation, usually with two spaces between paragraphs and with one space between each line.

collection letter: usually written by companies to other companies or to individual customers; attempts to motivate the payment of an overdue debt.

(*A follow-up collection letter* is written when the first brings no response from the debtor after a reasonable interlude.)

complaint letter: written by an individual customer or in behalf of a company; it recounts the facts of a grievance against a company and requests specific remedies from the company addressed.

complimentary close: placed two spaces below the last line of the body of a letter and lined up with the date; it precedes the written signature of the sender, is always followed by a comma, and always begins with a capital letter (if it contains more than one word, only the first letter of the first word is capitalized: Sincerely yours,).

condolence letter: written to a colleague or customer who is ill or who has had an accident: a *letter of sympathy* expresses sorrow to someone who has lost a close relative or friend. (Some people use *condolence letter* to mean a *letter of sympathy,* so it is best to ask what is wanted.)

congratulatory letter: written to a colleague or customer on such occasions as appointments, promotions, awards, elections.

cover letter: written to introduce the receiver to materials that are attached or which are being forwarded separately.

follow-up letter (after a job interview): written to thank someone for his/her time and, if appropriate, reaffirming interest in the position (also used in *collection letters* and in *sales letters*).

form letter: a standardized message composed by companies in advance of particular situations to replace individual replies because of the volume of correspondence. Its greatest shortcoming is that it may not be entirely appropriate to the situation at hand, but it gets sent anyway.

inquiry letter: addressed to companies and individuals, this letter usually asks for information (for example, whether or not someone is a good credit risk).

inside address: consisting of the name and address of the receiver of a letter, it is typed flush with the left margin, single-spaced between lines, and set off from the *salutation* by two spaces.

interoffice memoranda: messages (memos) sent and received *within* the same organization, they are generally concerned with one point of information or with a few closely related points.

minutes: a transcription in summary form of the content of a meeting taken by someone present at the meeting, it usually mentions the main points discussed, conclusions reached, votes taken, the names of people present at the meeting.

proposal: a draft of a plan submitted to an executive or to a foundation or agency; it is as detailed as possible in order to answer all questions that the receiver is likely to have.

reply letter: written to acknowledge the receipt of a request; should be written whether the request is approved or denied.

request letter: usually written to a company by another company or by an individual to obtain information, literature, or a sample of some product.

registered mail: mail recorded in the post office from which it is mailed and guaranteed special care in delivery; also a "return receipt" can be requested so that the sender has proof the material was recieved.

report: in business writing, reports of varying length are written for a specific audience for a particular purpose or to achieve a desired effect that is well thought out in advance.

résumé: means "summary" in French and lists, under appropriate headings, the work experiences, skills, educational background and perhaps even the achievements and career goals that would most interest a prospective employer.

resignation letter: written as a courtesy when one knows that one must leave a job; it should, if possible, be written at least two weeks before the resignation takes effect to insure good references.

return address: part of the heading of the letter; includes the address (not the name) of the sender, is single-spaced, and is followed by the date (the complimentary close is lined up under the return address).

sales letter: sent directly to a customer's home or to a company; its purpose is to get attention at once, then maintain it, and if possible, close by making clear what action the prospective customer should take.

salutation: to greeting line of a letter; it is set off by two paces from the inside address and is followed by two spaces before the beginning of the letter (for a business letter the form is Dear Ms. Johnson: and in an informal letter the form is Dear Mary,).

CHAPTER 42

Writing for Examinations

One of the most common kinds of tests that we take is called the objective test: multiple-choice items that have only one correct answer. However, there will be times when we will have to take *subjective* examinations, tests involving questions that require paragraphs and essays as appropriate responses. These tests are common in college courses; essays are also required by the Civil Service when it tests candidates for promotion; and many employment tests are in essay form as well. Writing paragraphs and essays for examinations forces you to demonstrate your knowledge of a problem or situation more than any single objective question ever can.

In writing paragraphs and essays for examinations, you can follow several basic steps to increase your chances of responding successfully to the questions.

1. *Read the entire examination carefully.*

Do not simply leap into the test. If you find the instructions confusing, or any question vague, ask the teacher or tester for an explanation. Not all examinations are prepared well; even if they are, the people who have designed them should be prepared to rephrase any question that perplexes you.

2. *Determine how many questions you must answer and how each question is weighted.*

If you must answer all questions, then plan to do so. If you have choices, be absolutely certain that the number of questions you must answer in each part of the examination (if there is more than one part) is clear. Moreover, check the numerical weight given to each question in the grading process. Plan to spend more time on the questions which carry the heaviest weight.

3. *Divide your time accordingly.*

If you must write three short paragraphs based on three questions, each weighted equally, within a fifty-minute period, then you obviously should plan to devote fifteen minutes to each question and use the five minutes left for proofreading. Try to adhere strictly to your time division. If you spend too much time on one question, and consequently are unable to handle the other questions, the instructor in all likelihood will *not* grant you any concessions.

4. *Start with the question that you feel most confident about.*

Always answer questions that you know you can handle quickly and competently. If you can complete at least one paragraph or essay ahead of your time schedule, you will be able to devote a few extra minutes to those questions that you anticipate some difficulty with. For each answer, develop a series of points that you plan to cover, or create a scratch outline. These procedures will help you to organize answers clearly.

5. *Proofread each answer as you complete it.*

If you leave all proofreading until the end in a very long exam, you might discover that you have run out of time. As you proofread, remember the need for correct spelling and grammatical accuracy, among other things. Do not assume that the tester is going to grade for content alone.

6. *Make certain that all necessary information is submitted with your examination.*

Quite possibly you will be writing your examination in college "blue books"—booklets designed especially for the writing of paragraphs and essays. List all the information—name, date, course, instructor—called for on the cover. If you use more than one blue book, number each in the following manner: "1 of 2," "2 of 2." Put one book inside the other before handing them in.

There is an additional aspect of the examination process that is of critical importance to you. In most essay questions, there is a *key word* that dictates the strategy that you must use in your written response. Look at the following examination questions, which have the key words underlined. Familiarize yourself with the meaning of these words.

Analyze "Song of Myself"   (*Analysis* means to separate something into its important parts in order to discover its nature, function, relationship.)

Classify *Freud's views on the human mind.*   (*Classify* means to divide into main sections for better understanding.)

Compare *Grant and Lee as Generals.*   (*Compare* means to treat likenesses.)

> *Hint:* Sometimes when a question asks you to write a comparative essay, the actual meaning is "compare *and* contrast." Make certain that you know what is required by the question.

Contrast *the Democratic and Republican parties.*   (*Contrast* means to point out differences.)

Criticize *the concept of the welfare state.*   (*Criticize* means to point out the good and bad aspects.)

Define *"tragedy."*   (*Define* means to explain the meaning of a term.)

Describe *an amoeba.*   (*Describe* means to name the features of something in terms of movement, space, position of its various parts, and the like.)

Discuss *the economic theory of supply and demand.*   (*Discuss* means to explain and to elaborate on a term or concept.)

Evaluate *your English course.*   (*Evaluate* means to present your opinion of the advantages and disadvantages or the good and bad features of something.)

Explain *internal combustion.*   (*Explain* means to tell about the workings or processes involved; to clarify.)

Illustrate *the forms of music popular with teenagers today.*   (*Illustrate* means to give one or more clear, relevant examples.)

Interpret *the Bill of Rights.*   (*Interpret* means to present the importance or meaning of something.)

List *several causes of juvenile delinquency.*   (*List* means to present a series of items without extensive discussion.)

Outline *the Industrial Revolution in America.*   (*Outline* means to give only the main points.)

Review *your favorite book.*   (*Review* means to examine thoroughly and provide specific comments.)

Summarize *the plot of a movie or television program that you dislike.*   (*Summarize* means to examine the main points and do it briefly.)

There are other key words—*state, name, diagram, prove, justify, relate, itemize*—that direct you toward what is called for in a question requiring a paragraph or essay. Know what these words mean, and frame your answers accordingly.

Essay examinations force you to remember what you have learned, to organize that knowledge, and quite often to provide your own ideas and insights. Essay questions on examinations test your ability to reason, your knowledge of facts, your understanding of a topic. Also tested is your ability to write with accuracy and grammatical correctness. Do not overlook the sound principles of word choice, sentence construction, and paragraph organization that have been stressed in earlier parts of this *Handbook*.

Application   Take one of the sample examination questions used to illustrate key words in this section and write a 100-word response to it in paragraph form. You have twenty minutes to complete this test. Budget your time accordingly.

_____

_____

_____

_____

_____

_____

_____

_____

_____

_____

_____

CHAPTER 43

Manuscript Preparation: Revising, Proofreading, and Submitting Written Work

Although you have handled many writing projects in this *Handbook,* there are probably few instances in which the very first version that you scratched out is the version that you gave to a teacher. You have a responsibility to submit your very best writing to a teacher, employer, or colleague. In order to prepare your manuscript (which is a written or typed paper) for submission, you have to revise and proofread your material.

43.1. Revising Papers

The process of revision begins with an awareness on your part that the first version of any piece of writing is not necessarily the one that will be submitted. For most people, including professionals, good writing involves the creation of a first draft, the revision of that draft, and perhaps additional revisions until the paper is as perfect as possible.

When you revise a paper, try to allow at least a day to elapse between the first draft and any revision. As you revise, consider the three main areas that teachers, employers, and others look at: content, organization, and writing. Address yourself to the following questions in each of these categories.

Content

a. Do you have enough material for the assignment? If you have to write a 250-word composition, then you should provide approximately that much writing.
b. Is your material fresh? No one likes to read material that simply is too

obvious or well known. Try to present ideas and details that are new, lively, or important.

c. Do you have enough details to support your generalizations? Remember that strings of generalizations create content that is simplistic, vague, and boring. Provide details and examples to support your generalizations.

Organization

a. Do you have a topic sentence and a clincher sentence for the paragraph? In the absence of a topic sentence, does the main idea emerge clearly from the paragraph?
b. Does your paragraph or essay have a clear beginning, middle, and end?
c. Does the paragraph or essay progress, or move forward, from point to point, or do you backtrack or repeat yourself too much?
d. Does your writing have unity and coherence (see pp. 149–152)? Could you eliminate anything that is unnecessary or that detracts from your writing?
e. Have you used the appropriate strategies (definition, classification, comparison and contrast, and so forth) to develop your paper?

Writing

a. Have you avoided common grammatical mistakes like fragments, comma splices, and faulty agreement?
b. Have you used correct punctuation and capitalization?
c. Have you used the right words to convey meanings accurately?
d. Have you avoided colloquialisms, slang, dialect, and other "spoken" forms, except for special effects?
e. Have you spelled all words correctly?
f. Have you varied your sentences and used coordination and subordination effectively?

43.2. Proofreading

Proofreading is the careful checking of the paper that you plan to submit to a teacher, friend, or employer. It differs from revision in that proofreading does not offer you the opportunity to totally rewrite the paper or make drastic changes in the content or organization. Proofreading is important in itself because it permits you a final opportunity to correct certain common mistakes that arise from carelessness, haste, or uncertainty during the writing process.

Here are some basic items to check when you proofread the final version of a paper:

1. Check the title. Are all important words capitalized?

Hint: Do not underline your title or put it in quotation marks.

---

2. Check all items that should be capitalized.
3. Check the spelling of any word you are uncertain about.
4. Check the meaning of any word that you think you might have misused.
5. Check to see if you have unintentionally omitted any words.
6. Check paragraph form. Have you indented each paragraph? Are there any sentences that are useless and can be crossed out neatly?
7. Check to make certain that you have smooth, correct sentences. This is your last chance to avoid awkward, incomplete, or grammatically incorrect sentences. Make your changes carefully in pen.

Talented proofreaders develop an ability to spot mistakes quickly as they scan a page of written or typed material. Perhaps you can develop similar talents. For now, read your material slowly and carefully for mistakes. Better still, read the material aloud. If something *sounds* wrong to you, consult an appropriate section in this *Handbook,* a dictionary, or another reference work. Then make corrections accordingly.

43.3. Guidelines for Submitting Written Work

Whether you are writing a paragraph or an essay, you should make an effort to submit material in as attractive a manner as possible. A neat paper has an edge over a sloppy one. Sometimes a teacher will refuse to accept a paper that is not prepared properly. To avoid this, observe the following guidelines for submitting written work:

1. Always use paper of a standard size—usually 8½ by 11 inches. This paper should always be white. If you are not typing your paragraph or essay, make certain that the paper you are using is lined. *Do not use paper torn from a notebook.*
2. Double-space the lines if you are typing. If you are writing the paper, ask the teacher if he or she wants you to write on alternate lines.
3. When writing a paper, always use pens with blue or black ink. Do not use other colors. Never submit a paper that is written in pencil.

4. Write or type on only one side of the page, unless the teacher permits writing on both sides.
5. Make certain that you have a margin on all sides of the paper. This margin should be at least one inch. If you are working at home, try to buy paper that has a vertical line on the left; this will serve as your left-hand margin.
6. Put your name, the name of the course, the name of the teacher, and the date at the top of the first page.
7. Number all pages at the top, either in the center or at the right-hand side.
8. Use a paperclip to fasten all pages securely.

INDEX